Ages and Stages

Ages and Stages

A Parent's Guide to Normal Childhood Development

Charles E. Schaefer

Theresa Foy DiGeronimo

John Wiley & Sons, Inc.

New York • Chichester • Weinheim • Brisbane • Singapore • Toronto

This book is printed on acid-free paper. ♾

Published by John Wiley & Sons, Inc.
Published simultaneously in Canada.

ISBN 0-471-37087-8

Printed in the United States of America.

V00170_050118

Contents

STAGE 2:
18 to 36 Months

STAGE 3:
36 Months to the Sixth Birthday

STAGE 4: *6 to 9 Years*

Introduction

Ages and Stages: A Parent's Guide to Normal Childhood Development has been written to help you answer these three questions as your child grows from birth to age 9:

- What behaviors can I expect at different ages and stages of development?
- How can I help my child advance to the next level of development?
- How can I tell when my child's development is outside the norm and requires professional intervention?

The answers that we offer to these questions are based on the latest scientific research regarding a child's emotional, cognitive, social, moral, and psychological development. This information is coupled with examples, stories, activities, and hands-on dos and don'ts that you can use immediately to positively influence your child's development through the years.

You'll find that the book is divided into four stages of child development: (1) birth to 18 months, (2) 18 to 36 months, (3) 36 months to the sixth birthday, and (4) 6 to 9 years. In each stage the same five areas of growth are explored. You will find information on: (1) emotional health, (2) cognitive development, (3) family and peer relationships, (4) personal growth, and (5) character formation. This structure of continuity allows you to watch the continuum of growth in your child. You can, for example, read about the role of fantasy in the life of a 2-year-old and read ahead to see how the use of fantasy in daily life will change when the child is 4. This format also lets you see the reasons for the emotional and psychological differences in siblings. You can see why the expression of anger by your 1-year-old is different from that of your 5-year-old. This format also shows you how your parenting strategies should change as your child ages; you will see, for example, why the way you handle peer pressure with a toddler is different from the way you handle it when a child is 9.

Of course, a child's development does not always proceed in a continuous upward course, but rather follows a jagged line, with peaks (growth spurts), valleys (regression to earlier stages), and plateaus (periods of no discernible growth). Still, a developmental course toward maturity can be generalized to illustrate what is normally expected at certain ages. This book is your guide to that development. It tells you what you can expect as your child grows, what you can be on the lookout for, and what you can influence in both positive and negative ways. It also alerts you to the red flags that indicate a child may need professional help or some other type of intervention in order to successfully move to the next level and reach his or her full potential.

We hope that *Ages and Stages* will be a clear and useful source of information for you throughout the years and that you will find it worn from use as your child leaves childhood behind and ventures into adolescence–where a whole new adventure begins.

Birth to 18 Months

STAGE 1

Dear Diary,

I can't believe that Christopher is already 18 months old. Will all his days and months and years with me zip by so quickly? It seems like such a short time ago that we brought him home as a newborn and stared for hours at his little face and wondered what the months ahead would bring.

It took a while for us to get to know each other. At first I jumped every time he let out the slightest whimper; I wanted him to know that he could count on me to keep him comfortable and safe. It wasn't long before all my efforts were rewarded with his wonderful smiles, and then came those delicious, wet kisses, and now his famous bear hugs. When he was only about 6 months old, I remember the way his whole face would light up and his big nearly toothless smile would greet me when I picked him up out of his crib every morning. What a wonderful way to start each day. I don't mean to sound like we haven't had our tough times, too. There've been lots of days when Christopher has let us all know that he's not completely happy with the way we're taking care of him. Right from when he was an infant, he'd hold his breath and then scream when he felt frustrated—not too much has changed in that department.

I think I'm still his favorite person (if I do say so myself). At around 7 months old, Christopher decided he didn't want anyone but me to hold him when he was tired, and he definitely didn't want to stay with a babysitter (even his dad couldn't calm him down sometimes when I went out). He's getting better now about staying with other people, but he still likes it best when I'm around (especially if there's a loud noise or a big dog around; they seem to frighten him).

Would I be bragging too much if I said that I think Christopher is a very smart little boy? He has always been the kind of person who focuses intently on things and tries to figure everything out. I remember even when he was just 4 months old or so how he'd hold things, look at them so closely (and of course put everything in his mouth to explore the feel and texture). Around 8 months, he spent so much time with his crib activity board, pushing the buttons, spinning the wheels, and figuring out how everything worked over and over again. He has always loved to go places—he seems eager to see everything and learn about every twig, leaf, and ladybug he passes. It's just amazing to watch his thinking skills in action. Lately I've noticed that he seems to enjoy pretending—he sits in a box and pretends it's a car. He picks up a stick and pretends it's an airplane. He's so much fun—and now that he can talk a bit, I have a better idea of what he's thinking. It's incredible that a child can move from babbling sounds like bababa at 6 months old to saying, "I want juice" just one year later. Right now, his favorite word is no!

It's been fascinating to watch Christopher become a part of our family. At first he was just this totally dependent little human being who didn't know us at all and only cared that he was fed and dry. Then he began to recognize us and reach out to be held and played with. Pretty soon he was "talking" up a storm, using his own little lan-

guage to tell me all about his day and his dreams and plans. Now he seems so grown up as he plays with his little friends (or plays next *to them, I should say, because they don't seem to get the idea of socializing yet). He no longer is the totally dependent infant who needed me to do everything for him—he's growing up to be a confident and sometimes-independent little person.*

I want Christopher to learn how to share, and how to be kind, and how to understand the needs of others, but he just isn't ready yet—my wonderful, beautiful son is very self-centered right now. Because he's sure the world revolves around him, he just doesn't seem to care about the feelings of others. He doesn't share at all. He sometimes hits his friends. And it's like talking to the wall when I try to explain why he has to clean up his own toys. I think all I can do right now is to show him through my own example and with facial expressions and my tone of voice what is right and wrong, good and bad. Hopefully, in the next few months he'll get the idea.

Emotional Health

Although many forces shape a child's level of emotional competence (such as genetics and environmental factors), it is now well known that the parent–child relationship during infancy and toddlerhood has an exceptionally strong and lifelong influence on children's emotional development. In fact, there is growing biological evidence that infants need responsive care from their parents and caretakers in order for the parts of their brains that control emotions to develop properly. This development is nurtured as infants learn about love and affection, joy and anger, and fear.

Love and Affection

Eight-month-old Rachel sat contentedly in her infant seat watching her grandmother prepare her lunch. Then, suddenly, Rachel came alive as if someone had thrown a switch in her nervous system. Her face lit up with a full-face smile, her arms flailed up and down, and her little legs kicked wildly as she let out a loud squeal. The love of her life had just entered the room—Mom was home.

Making children feel loved is the single most important task of parenting. This feeling enables children to value and love themselves. It teaches them how to love and relate to other people. And it allows them to become emotionally stable persons. Our children learn to love by being loved. It's as simple as that.

Love and affection are first nurtured in infants through the development of trust. From the moment of birth, children begin the task of assessing if they can trust the world they live in to meet their needs. Are cries for food promptly answered or are they ignored for long periods? Is the need for comfort lovingly met or is it answered with harsh words and rough handling? Do they have influence over the adults who care for them or are they powerless in an indifferent world? The answers to these questions determine how emotionally secure children grow and how they later form attachments of love and affection.

Babies who learn that the adults in their lives are trustworthy and can be counted on to respond to cries of frustration or distress form a positive image of themselves and others. Parents who can respond with a soft voice to a baby's hunger at 3 A.M. or respond to a baby's persistent cries with gentle handling (even when they themselves are fatigued and impatient) teach children that they are important and loved. This lesson allows children to later build loving relationships. But if babies learn that their cries for help are not answered or result in anger or harsh treatment, they become wary and distrustful of others. As these children grow they generally lack confidence and feel unworthy of warm, responsive attention.

AGE DIFFERENCES

For the first 6 months, infants do not feel love and affection. They are wholly dependent on their caretakers to have their needs met—that's all. In the second half of the first year, babies become attached to their primary caregivers and begin to show much affection by kissing and hugging. In the second year, most babies are head-over-heels in love with their parents.

To an infant, love means development of affectional attachment with a caretaker. This relationship (called *attachment* or *bonding*) becomes firmly established by the time the infant is 8

CONSIDER

With approximately 6 million infants and toddlers in childcare in the United States, it's very important that the caregivers know the importance of love and affection. To promote healthy emotional development, infant childcare should have the following characteristics:

- **Warm, sensitive caregivers who are trained in infant development, who understand the importance of children's early relationships, and who are able to form effective partnerships with parents.**
- **Low staff turnover, to ensure continuity in caregiving for children.**
- **Small groups of 6 to 8 infants or 8 to 10 toddlers.**
- **Low child-teacher ratios: no more than three (and for high-risk children, preferably two) infants per adult. Each infant should be assigned to only one or two primary caregivers who feed, change, and play with the babies, allowing the babies to form meaningful, secure relationships with those who care for them. Caregivers should not change each year (any more than we would recommend changing parents every year) but should stay with the same infants for at least 3 years (Lally & Gordon, 1977).**

SEX DIFFERENCES

Bonding is not for mothers and infants only. Children attach themselves to many people, depending on the nature of their long-term interactions. This leaves the door wide open to secure attachments between the child and the father. Fathers who make an effort to spend time with their babies, who talk and laugh and play with them, teach their children that they are someone special who can be counted on to give lots of love and attention. This is the foundation of attachment. Babies typically develop an attachment to a second caretaker (often the father) by 18 months of age.

or 9 months of age and is characterized by strong interdependence, intense mutual feelings, and vital emotional ties. Early attachment helps a child develop trust and confidence in the caregiver and is vital to the quality of relationships the person will later develop with peers, relatives, other adults, and a spouse.

Bonding does not happen immediately, or quickly, or in only a given window of time. It is a process that happens over many months and even years. Like any other love relationship, it develops in gradual stages and improves and deepens with time and attention.

If you want your baby to "love" you, try these three simple suggestions:

- Consistently and immediately respond to your baby's cries of distress.
- Give much physical contact. Babies feel safer, sleep better, gain more weight, and are more interested in being with people when they are often cuddled, held, and stroked. The importance of loving touch cannot be overemphasized.
- Play with your baby. Even in the first few months of life, infants enjoy games like peek-a-boo and songs. This creates a pleasure bond that encourages affectional attachment.

JUST A PHASE?

If a baby does not show signs of attachment to the primary caretaker by 1 year of age, the parent should seek a consultation with a pediatric mental health professional.

Some signs that an infant is making this affectional attachment to you are the following:

- The baby will smile when he or she sees you.
- The baby will seek close physical contact with you when he or she is distressed.

SCIENCE TO TAKE HOME

Some infants are more securely attached to their parents than others. Researchers Ainsworth, Bell, and Stayton observed mothers and their babies at home and noticed that mothers of securely attached infants ages 9 to 11 months were especially sensitive to their children's efforts to signal their needs and quicker to respond to those needs than were mothers of insecurely attached children. This "fit" between the mother's and the infant's behaviors has been called *synchrony*, and in numerous studies throughout the years it has been found to be a strong indicator of overall attachment quality (Hughes, Noppe, & Noppe, 1996).

- The baby will be upset when separated from you.
- The baby will show pleasure when reunited with you.

Parenting to Nurture Love and Affection

- Teach your child to trust you by responding consistently with love and sensitivity to your baby's cries of hunger, pain, or discomfort.
- If you need childcare, find a program that allows one caregiver to take care of your child over a long period of time.
- Create an affectional attachment with your baby by (1) consistently and immediately responding to your baby's cries of distress, (2) giving much physical contact, and (3) playing with your baby.
- Make your baby feel safe and comfortable.

Avoid

- Getting angry when your child begins to cling to you and avoid strangers at around 8 months of age. It is a normal sign of attachment and affection.
- Letting your own fatigue or anger push you to respond negatively to your baby's cries.
- Assuming your infant doesn't need quality time with you because he or she seems content to be alone.
- Expecting bonding to happen immediately, or quickly, or in only a given window of time. It is a process that happens over many months and even years.

REMEMBER

Love and affection is a give-and-take proposition. What you give to your baby is what your baby learns to give back to you.

Joy and Anger

Although the emotions of joy and anger are very much a part of babyhood, most child experts believe that these feelings require mental processes that are not present at birth. Parents may swear that their newborns light up with joy one minute and have a quick temper the next, but the smiles and cries are actually prompted by other, internal stimuli.

Joy

The smile of a newborn is probably based on brain stem activity. It occurs during rapid eye movement (REM) sleep and during those waking states in which rapid eye movements can also be discerned. Then, between 1½ to 2½ months, smiles begin to appear when the baby sees something pleasing. Social smiling begins around 2½ to 3 months; at this time, familiar faces are more likely to elicit smiles than nonfamiliar ones, indicating that early smiling already has a cognitive component involving memory. Between 3 and 5 months, babies will smile when they notice they can control their environment; they will smile, for example, when they learn they can make a mobile move by vigorously kicking their legs. (This is called *mastery motivation;* the pleasure of success encourages them to try harder and stick to a task longer.)

Smiling may turn to outright laughter by 4 months, indicating great pleasure and a feeling of delight. At first, this laughter occurs mainly as a result of physical stimulation such as tickling, but by the second half of the first year the baby will laugh in response to interesting or incongruous events. (See the "Play and Imagination" section under "Cognitive Development" later in Stage 1.)

By the end of the first year and during the second, sustained joy or elation can be seen in toddlers. They show particular pleasure when anticipating events that will occur and in planning such events. They'll giggle themselves silly, for example, when they know in advance that you're going to jump out from your hiding place and say, "Boo!"

Whatever prompts a baby's smile, it is surely nature's way of gaining the child positive attention. Who can resist responding to a baby's smile with a smile in return? A child's laughter is rewarded with reciprocal laughing, talking, and other kinds of positive attention from adults. This teaches socialization skills by encouraging the child to smile and laugh some more.

Anger

Feelings of anger develop in much the same way as feelings of joy. In the beginning, infant crying is a call for relief from distress; it is not a display of anger. But by 6 months, anger is evident in response to frustration. When you restrict your child's body movements while dressing, bathing, or buckling up the car seat, for example, you'll see frustration turn into angry flailing of arms and legs.

Babies also feel frustrated because they are totally dependent on someone else to give them everything they desire–a helpless situation that prompts anger. Nine-month-old Jacob pushed forcefully away from his mother as he reached out toward something he wanted across the room. Jacob squirmed, twisted, and cried, but he couldn't make his mother understand what he wanted. "I've noticed," says his mom, "that Jacob gets very frustrated when he can't do things for himself. He just can't wait to grow up."

Anger is also an enabling emotion. It energizes and motivates babies to keep trying to master a frustrating event. Babies soon learn that anger can prompt action; it gains attention; it wields some power. For example, 16-month-old Clara jangled her mother's keys with glee, but then began to scream when her mom took them away. The anger grew not only from frustration, but also because past experiences had taught Clara that her anger would keep her mother's attention and would probably bring back the keys.

Now is a good time to begin teaching your child about anger by letting her experience it and by resisting the temptation to always jump to remove the frustration. If your child's temper flares because he can't make the jack-in-the-box pop up, let him struggle with it for just a bit. Babies need to learn about anger in a safe, protected environment.

CONSIDER

The line between joy and anger is a thin one for a young child. One moment your baby may be laughing out loud, and with the next breath the laugh becomes a heartbreaking scream. This line is drawn at the point of overstimulation. What is fun for 5 minutes may be more than the baby's developing nervous system can take for 5½ minutes. When your baby is laughing and having a great time, look for signs that a meltdown is about to occur. Babies will yawn, turn their face away from you, rub their eyes, or begin to wave their arms in frustration.

Through experience they learn that it's okay to be angry, that it's a natural response, and they learn how to let it go when it doesn't get them what they want. Experience with anger teaches children emotional control. Situations such as waiting for food or sitting in a car seat provide important opportunities for acquiring regulation skills such as turning away from the frustrating object, distracting oneself with something more comforting (like a favorite toy), and engaging in self-soothing activities (such as holding a favorite blanket or sucking fingers). Research indicates that infants who have not learned how to regulate their angry feelings are more likely to be noncompliant with parental directions when they get older and are thus likely to experience behavioral problems. But children who do learn how to deal with anger early on are better prepared when they reach school age and their parents aren't there to save the day when they encounter situations that make them angry.

It's never too early to help children learn about joy and anger by giving the feelings a name. You may feel silly telling a red-faced, screaming 9-month-old that he or she looks mad, but the idea is to get in the habit of connecting words to internal feelings. When you smile, tell your baby, "I feel so happy." Emotions have to be identified and named for children. When they understand that their feelings have names, they begin to feel a sense of mastery over them.

Parenting to Help Children Handle Joy and Anger

- Have fun with your baby. Leave lots of time for laughing and playing.
- Let your baby watch you and family members having a good time together.
- If your baby can't stand being held down for safe diapering, provide

---

SCIENCE TO TAKE HOME

Mark E. Cummings of the National Institute of Mental Health Lab of Developmental Psychology in Bethesda, Maryland, studied young children's responses to expressions of anger by family members. He found that by 1 year of age, children are not only aware of others' anger, but they are also likely to react to it emotionally with feelings of stress and a threatened sense of security. So hold your temper in front of your baby. Right from infancy, your child learns about anger control by watching and imitating family members (Cummings, 1989).

---

a pacifier or a toy to reduce the frustration of being unwillingly restricted.

- Control your own short fuse. Don't model behavior you don't want your child to imitate.
- Let your baby experience controlled amounts of frustration and anger.

Avoid

- Denying the emotion of anger. Your goal is not to repress or destroy your child's angry feelings, but rather to help your child accept the feelings and channel and direct them to constructive ends.
- Hiding your anger when your child does something wrong (like intentionally biting you or smashing a glass on the floor) for fear your child won't love you. Children need to see that anger is a natural response to distress.
- Holding a grudge. After an angry outburst you need to show your child how to reestablish a positive relationship.
- Verbally or physically abusing your child–ever. This hurts your child's sense of self-esteem and damages your relationship with your child.
- Trying to protect your child from all frustration. It is an important developmental skill to learn how to deal with angry feelings.

REMEMBER

A baby's smile is nature's way of guaranteeing that babies receive positive attention. When your baby smiles and laughs and you do the same, your baby is learning how to socialize and interact with others.

A baby quickly learns that anger is an enabling emotion that can prompt action, gain attention, and wield some power. Babies shouldn't be completely sheltered from this emotion.

Managing Fear

In early infancy, babies form close bonds of love and trust with important and familiar people, especially their parents. They learn to feel comfortable and secure with the world around them. Putting their well-being completely in the hands of another, they have few fears. Very young babies can be left alone in the dark, brought to high places, shown large animals or small insects, and handed off to strangers–all without a fearful reaction.

Then one day, somewhere between the sixth and eighth month, most babies become very anxious when confronted by strangers. Your baby has become familiar with the few faces he or she sees daily and has learned to distinguish these

JUST A PHASE?

When your child shows symptoms of stranger anxiety, don't read too much into this behavior. Turning away from strangers, refusing to smile at Uncle Hank, running from the room when a non-family member enters are all very natural reactions to "strangers" in children under 18 months. This does not indicate the kind of social personality your child will have as an adult. It simply means that the person is unfamiliar and that your baby is reacting with caution. That's all.

faces from others. The degree of fear a baby feels when "new" faces enter the picture varies from child to child. You may notice one day that she buries her face in your chest when you try to show her off to your boss. Or, at the other extreme, you may be embarrassed when your mother-in-law reaches out to hold her and your formerly loving child lets loose with an ear-splitting scream of terror. You, too, can look like a stranger to your baby and send him into a crying jag if you do something to change your appearance. A new haircut, a pair of sunglasses, or the addition or loss of a mustache or beard on Dad can all set off an attack of stranger anxiety.

The key to helping babies deal with stranger anxiety is to understand their fear and to give them emotional support rather than an angry scolding. Babies are still too young to learn lessons about courage and self-reliance. They certainly have no interest in being polite to strangers who want to whisk them away from their mothers' arms. They need to know they can cling to you and you won't betray them by insisting they sit on a "stranger's" lap. Ignore anyone who tells you not to cater to your child's fear. At this age, the best thing you can do is to let your baby meet many new people from the security of your protective arms or even from behind your legs. When you approach someone who is not familiar to your child, watch your demeanor. If you tense up, use a low or harsh voice, or appear unhappy, your baby will immediately become fearful. Instead, keep your voice light and positive. Smile. When you're relaxed, you communicate to your child that the situation is safe and the newcomer is friendly.

CONSIDER

Never sneak out of the house to avoid a separation scene with your baby. This will undermine basic trust in you and will trigger greater separation anxiety in the future.

The next fear you may notice in your baby stems from separation anxiety. Babies can't grasp the concept of permanence just yet. As far as babies know, when you move out of sight, you're gone forever. That's why from about 10 months of age, your baby will begin to cry when you leave the room; he'll cling to your leg; she'll scream when you try to leave the house. Your baby is afraid he or she will never see you again.

Knowing this fear of separation is perfectly normal doesn't make it any easier to bear. Some parents avoid the screaming scenes by choosing to never leave their babies. This is impractical for most parents and impedes the growth of self-reliance in the child. Although most children begin to outgrow separation anxiety by 18 months, you can teach your child now that separation is not permanent.

Separation games can help. When your baby is awake, say bye-bye, leave the room for a brief period of time, and then return with a smile and offer a cuddle. Do this often throughout the day, extending the amount of time you're out of sight each time. (If your baby immediately cries when you leave the room, try maintaining voice contact while you're out of sight.) Games of peek-a-boo and hide-and-seek are also playful ways to teach the reassuring reality of object permanence. More difficult, but also instructive, are short periods of separation. Leave your baby with a trusted (and familiar) caregiver while you drive yourself around the block a few times or run an errand. Wear a smile and an upbeat attitude both when you leave (despite the

SCIENCE TO TAKE HOME

A parent's influence on a baby's perception of fear has been well documented. A classic study reported in *Emotion: Theory, Research and Experience,* Volume 2 (Klinnert, Campos, & Sorce, 1983), offers a vivid example. In this study, a 6-month-old boy was placed on a special table on which the edge had been extended with a clear piece of firm plastic. When the child crawled to the edge of the natural table, he looked over it, appeared to perceive the apparent drop-off, and stopped before attempting to crawl further. Once stopped, he automatically turned and looked for his mother. On seeing her, he specifically focused on her face. If the mother showed a facial expression of fear, he would invariably maintain his hesitation and not go forward. However, when the mother smiled as he looked at her, he would invariably crawl over the natural edge of the table. This study reinforces the belief that infants use the emotional communications of their parents to determine if they are afraid (Gemelli, 1996).

crying child on your leg) and when you return. Doing this several times a week teaches your child that you do return and that separation is nothing to fear.

After 6 months, babies may also develop fears of things in their environment. The loud noise of the vacuum cleaner or of thunder may scare them. Large animals, fireworks, and clowns may scare them silly. These fears are rooted in the strange, the unexpected, and the unmanageable. If your child develops such a fear, try to desensitize his or her response. If it's the vacuum cleaner, for example, let him play with and get acquainted with the machine while it's unplugged. Show him the on/off switch so he sees you control it. Hold him in your arms at a comfortable distance while someone else turns it on briefly. For fear of dogs, let her watch a movie or read her a book about a child and a loving dog. Give her a soft, cuddly toy dog to play with. Introduce her to a very small dog from a few feet away. Slowly let her decide when she's comfortable about getting close to the object of her fear.

Parenting to Help Children Handle Fear

- Respect your child's fears. Expecting a child to be "tough" only makes the child more anxious.
- Acknowledge and show understanding of the fear by saying something like, "I know loud noises can be scary."
- Praise your child for any effort, no matter how small, to overcome a fear.
- Assure your child that you will keep him or her from harm.
- Remember that all children have an innate fear of the unknown and the unmanageable.

Avoid

- Overdoing your support. Too much coddling may convince your child that there really is something to be afraid of.
- Introducing the idea of fear. Saying "Don't be afraid" can make fear an option that the child hadn't even thought of.
- Calling your children's fears "silly." They are very real and serious to your child.

REMEMBER

Babies' fears of strangers, of separation, and of the strange, the unexpected, and the unmanageable are all natural developmental stages. They are best conquered with time and understanding. Parents need to recognize the stages in their children's lives at which they will be particularly prone to fears and anxiety.

- Threatening a punishment based on your child's fear. Saying "If you don't behave, I'm going to leave you in this store," for example, creates a new fear of abandonment.
- Expecting your child to think the way you do. Your child is inexperienced in this world and has no way of knowing that a loud siren cannot hurt her.

Cognitive Development

Did you know that the brain is the most immature organ at birth? That it continues to grow and develop during the first years of life? The dramatic impact of these truths is just now being realized as recent advances in brain research discover that the health of the brain is influenced not only by genetics, but also by life experiences. Interactions with other people and objects are such vital nutrients for the growing brain that they can literally cause the brain to develop in different ways.

This is both good and bad news. According to research compiled by the National Center for Infants, Toddlers, and Families, while good early experiences help the brain to develop well, poor early experiences can cause a genetically normal child to become mentally retarded or cause a temperamentally easygoing child to develop serious emotional difficulties (Hawley, 1998b).

Within each area of the brain there are millions of *neurons*, or nerve cells, which are connected to each other by *synapses*. These trillions of synapses and the pathways that they form make up the "wiring" of the brain, allowing all areas of the brain to communicate with each other. Neurons develop rapidly before birth, but after birth no new neurons are formed. Instead, brain development after birth consists of an ongoing process of wiring and rewiring the connections among neurons. New synapses between cells are constantly being formed while others are broken or pruned away. Early stimulating experiences can have a dramatic impact on this process, causing the final number of synapses in the brain to increase or decrease by as much as 25 percent (Hawley, 1998b).

These scientific facts explain why parents have such a profound influence on a child's cognitive development. Infants and children who are rarely spoken to, who are exposed to few toys, and who have little opportunity to explore and experiment with their environment may fail to fully develop the neural connections and pathways that facilitate later learning. Despite their normal genetic makeup, these children are at a permanent intellectual disadvantage. On the other hand, children who are given many opportunities to explore, experiment, and interact with others develop beyond their genetic programming.

Problem Solving

Babies learn to solve problems every time they touch, smell, see, feel, and taste the world around them. But they are unable to show any problem-solving skills until around the age of 6 months. At this time you can watch the development of a child's thinking skills that form the foundation for the complex process of problem solving in simple, everyday accomplishments:

- The 6- to 7-month-old has a collective memory that enables her to remember that a ball stays put even when it's covered by a blanket and that shaking a rattle makes a wonderful sound.
- The 8- to 9-month-old becomes fascinated with manipulating crib activity boards. He loves to push objects off the high chair just for the joy of watching what happens.
- The 10- to 12-month-old has increased memory skills and attention span allowing her to stay with an activity for 15 minutes and to remember daily routines.
- The 12- to 18-month-old learns to talk, to feed, dress, and wash himself, and even to laugh by imitating others.

AGE DIFFERENCES

You can stretch cognitive abilities by offering new age-appropriate toys and by challenging your baby's powers of observation with a varied environment. In infancy, change the color, shape, and texture of your baby's toys often. At about 6 months of age, offer toys that challenge thinking skills, such as shape sorters and ring towers (these stimulate concentration and eye-hand coordination). Don't let your 5-month-old become too content with the simple rattle that was thrilling at 3 months. After 6 months, change your baby's viewpoint by moving the high chair to a new spot and by rearranging the bedroom furniture. When your child is ready to "read," make a habit of reading picture books that pop up or offer textured pictures. Each new observation builds on the last and moves your baby forward confident in his or her ability to learn about the world.

In the second year, you will see signs that your baby is learning how to solve problems. Initially, problems are remedied through experimentation and by accident. For example, your baby may try to push a toy through the bars of her crib and find that, in the position she is holding it, the toy doesn't fit through. Eventually, by chance, she may turn the toy and succeed at pushing it through the crib slats. The next time she tries this "trick" she will remember to hold the toy in the correct position. Puzzles with large wooden pieces offer opportunities for this same kind of problem-solving experimentation. Babies will slide the pieces around the puzzle frame until they finally fall into place. They learn the correct position by accident, but retain the piece of information for the next time they try the puzzle. This accidental learning is the basis of future problem solving.

Because problem-solving skills so often develop through trial and error, your baby needs opportunities to try, fail, and try again. This willingness to persist at a task and struggle through difficulties is the key to anyone's ability to solve any problem. This ability to persist is first learned in babyhood *if* parents can resist being overindulgent. Some babies over the age of 6 months never have to struggle to figure out how to get a toy that is out of reach, or how to get food to their own mouths using a spoon, or how to clearly communicate their needs. Their parents are always nearby to remove all obstacles. These overprotected children have no opportunity learn how to think for themselves. If you want your baby to learn how to solve problems, allow him to have some problems to solve. Hide his ball under a blanket and encourage him to find it. When a toy is out of reach, give him some time to think of ways to get it himself. When he shows that he wants to try to do something himself, let him try (even when you know you can do it better and faster).

SCIENCE TO TAKE HOME

Children of overindulgent parents have had many, many frustrating situations removed from their experience, and they often come into adolescence ill-equipped for the frustrations of real life. As children they instead master strategies for getting the parent to resolve the frustration for them. They have tantrums or lose control emotionally when a task is experienced as difficult. They withdraw from the activity or give up, in hopes the parent will take over (Ellis, 1995).

Parenting to Build Problem-Solving Skills

- Offer opportunities to observe the world. Go outside, visit new places, and take a tour of the neighborhood.
- Let your baby watch family activities such as cooking meals, talking on the phone, and doing laundry. You think they're boring; your baby thinks they're fascinating.
- Give things names. Tell your infant, "This *ball* is *round*"; "Look at the *cat*." Tell your toddler, "I think you feel *sad*"; "Mary is your *friend*."
- Repeat favorite activities. Babies learn by repetition and will indicate when they're bored. If your child likes to hear the same story every night, don't fight it.
- Let your child try to work things out before you jump in to help.
- Let your child feel the pride of accomplishing something without your help

REMEMBER

Babies are unable to show any problem-solving skills until around the age of 6 months. After this time you can watch the development of a child's thinking skills that form the foundation for the complex process of problem solving in simple, everyday accomplishments.

Avoid

- Overstimulating your baby. Respect his need to pace his fun.
- Removing all obstacles from your baby's path. Let her think about how to solve a problem for herself.
- Protecting your child from all frustration. Problem solving requires a willingness to work through a task despite difficulty.
- Bringing out the flash cards in a misguided attempt to increase your baby's problem-solving skills. Far better to offer pots, pans, measuring spoons, water, plastic bowls, and cardboard boxes to encourage your child to think.

Play and Imagination

Play is the occupation of children. It is what allows them to grow emotionally, intellectually, and socially. Play teaches children how the world works and how they fit into it. Obviously, play is an important part of your baby's day.

In infancy, babies play through observation. It's fun for them to see new things and have frequent changes of scenery. They love to hear you sing songs. They like to watch you demonstrate how a rattle makes noise and can be held in the hand. You can guide your baby's fingers over the soft texture of stuffed animals. Gently tickle and kiss your baby's tummy and feet. All of these things help your baby learn how to interact with others for fun—after all, that's what play really is.

A major factor in children's play is imagination, but children are not born with an active imagination; it is something that grows gradually. Pretend play begins at the same time a child begins to speak (usually between 12 and 18 months, but occasionally sooner). The first signs will be fleeting: lifting a toy cup to the mouth or a toy telephone to the ear. These simple games will then progress to more sustained sequences such as feeding a beloved doll, washing a teddy bear's face, or sitting inside a cardboard "house."

These pretend moments encourage language development. Language uses words to represent real-life objects; so when your child makes a shoebox represent a car, he or she is developing the ability to

---

SCIENCE TO TAKE HOME

Moms and dads have different play styles. Researchers Biller and Meredith observed that mothers and fathers interact differently with their babies when they explore the environment. Here are some things they found:

- **Fathers encourage their babies' curiosity and, more specifically, actively encourage them to solve physical and intellectual challenges, even past the early signs of frustration. Mothers, on the other hand, while encouraging exploration, tend to be more conservative once the baby or toddler shows signs of frustration; they move in sooner than fathers to help the child or to remove some obstacle.**
- **Fathers tend to teach young children through the course of daily life activities. Mothers tend to engage with infants and toddlers in more toy-mediated types of play and learning.**
- **Fathers are more rough-and-tumble with their play. Children seem to enjoy the tactile and sensory aspects of physical interaction with Dad and will use his body as a jungle gym. Mothers, whose own bodies have often felt more than sufficiently used by their offspring (particularly if they have been breastfeeding), tend to avoid rough play. Babies wisely seek it less from Mom and head for Dad, the more willing partner (Pruett, 1997).**

JUST A PHASE?

Some parents worry if their child shows no interest in pretend play. They see other infants happily building sand castles or playing with dolls and wonder why their child wants no part in pretending. If your child seems to have no imagination, be patient for now. Children develop their creative personalities at various stages of infancy. At this time, your child may be more interested in exploring the environment or learning to crawl, walk, run, or jump. Continue to offer creative opportunities and toys and do some imaginative modeling and soon you'll likely see signs of a budding imagination.

think in terms of signs and symbols. Repetition of these actions gives young children confidence that they can create a play world that reflects real-life experiences.

At this age, children would rather invent their own games than explore a manufactured high-tech creation. Touching, tasting, and banging are typical means of playing and learning for babies and toddlers who are just finding out what the world is made of and what they can do. That's why some of the best toys for children this age are either ordinary household objects (pots, pans, wooden spoons, and spools) or children's versions of adult tools. If you do choose a high-tech toy for your tot, make sure it's one that gives your child as much latitude as possible in dictating the form of play, rather than one that has only one predetermined outcome.

SCIENCE TO TAKE HOME

One-year-old infants whose mothers allow them to take the lead during play interactions show more persistence at solving tasks a year later than infants whose mothers are more controlling (Frodi, Bridges, & Grolnick, 1985).

Parenting to Encourage Play and Imagination

- Play with your baby right from the start. Young infants love to dance in your arms and hear you sing songs. Wave to them, blow a kiss, smile often—they will soon surprise you by imitating your actions.
- Older infants love the anticipation of a surprise. Try the gonna-get-ya game as a quick way to reconnect after being apart: Wiggle your finger in the air as you musically say, "IIIIII'm gonna get ya!" As you say "gonna get ya," gently poke your baby's tummy.
- All the old-time baby games are still lots of fun. Don't forget peek-a-boo, pat-a-cake, this little piggy went to market, and the itsy-bitsy spider.

- To build a child's imagination provide lots of toys (like toy telephones and teacups) that encourage creative play.
- Model imaginative play yourself. For example, pretend to feed your child's stuffed animals.
- Be sure to applaud and smile at your child's beginning ventures into the world of play and imagination.

Avoid

- Misjudging your child's personality. By the second or third month you may notice that your baby is highly excitable and loves loud, aggressive play. Or, she may be more mellow and prefer quiet, soft play.
- Overstimulation. When your baby gives you the signal that he has had enough, end the playtime.
- Using play to distract your baby from tiredness or hunger. Those needs must be taken care of before a baby can enjoy playful interaction.
- Squashing your child's imagination by insisting on realism at all times. If she calls her stuffed bear a puppy dog, don't automatically correct her. If he insists on wearing one red sock and one white sock, give in when you can.
- Letting unsupervised siblings play with an infant. They can very easily (and unintentionally) harm a baby. It would not be unusual for a 3-year-old to wonder if a spoon inserted into one ear could come out the other side.
- Leaving family pets alone in the room with a baby. They do not know how to play with an infant.

REMEMBER

- **Play is the occupation of children. It is what allows them to grow emotionally, intellectually, and socially.**
- **Children are not born with an active imagination; it is something that grows gradually.**

Language Development

Language development doesn't begin the day your baby first says a word. It begins right from birth. Throughout their early months, babies are listening and learning constantly. They quickly learn words through repetition, tone of voice, and association, and they will respond to words long before they can actually speak them. Words like *bottle, mommy, daddy,* and *no* are usually part of a child's listening vocabulary by 7 months of age. By the time babies turn 1, they'll have about 20 words in their listening vocabulary, and then the rush of new spoken words daily begins. (*Listening vocabulary* means the words a person understands when someone else speaks them. These words may not yet be in the person's own speaking vocabulary.)

Unfortunately, some parents still feel silly talking to a child who gives no indication that he or she can understand or has any interest in the conversation. But by talking to babies and identifying objects like *bottle, crib,* and *stroller,* parents help them learn how to talk. It's not at all silly to say to a 1-month-old child, "I'm putting you in your stroller now and we're going for a walk to the park." Or, "This is our car. Mommy and Ben go for rides in the car." Let others laugh if they must; you're giving your baby one of the most important tools in cognitive growth: the gift of words.

I've heard parents say, "All of a sudden, one day, he just started talking!" The truth is, the growth of language is a constant thing–if you're listening for it. The progression of speech development outlined here will give you an approximation of how your baby learns how to talk (Barclay, 1985):

1. *Birth.* Crying is the sole means of communication used by newborns. With some experience, many parents can distinguish between the sounds of different cries–the cry for food, the cry for sleep, and the cry from frustration. The most important aspect of crying as communication is the fact that it causes the parent or

---

AGE DIFFERENCES

As in most other areas of development, babies learn language at different rates and in different ways. Some coo pleasantly; others grunt and squeak. Some babble incessantly; others listen intently. Some say their first word at 7 months; others wait until well into their second or third year. And even then, language development doesn't follow a linear path; children tend to take two steps forward and then one step back. They forget words they once knew so well. Sometimes, they stop talking altogether for a while. And the proper use of words like *ran* and *went* can suddenly become *runned* and *goed.* There is no definite timeline your child must follow in the pursuit of language development. All information based on age is offered only as a guideline to give a general idea of what can be expected of many children at certain ages.

---

adult to respond and thus fosters very early interaction. Also, newborns show great sensitivity to the human voice. Many are more responsive to higher-pitched voices, which may explain why they sometimes cry when Dad says a simple hello. If the father seems to be "scaring" the baby, he might try raising his voice an octave or two when he speaks.

2. *1 to 3 months.* It's time for cooing! Babies begin to make a noise that sounds like a pigeon cooing. When they are content and satisfied, they seem to make this sound just for the fun of it. Quite naturally, parents respond to this sound with a big smile. They may mimic the sound back and initiate "cooing conversations," or they may say (in a high-pitched, happy voice) something like, "Oohh, what are you trying to tell me? Are you happy today?" This kind of positive reaction makes the baby want to repeat the sound and gain more attention.
3. *2 to 7 months.* Vocal experimentation may become a baby's favorite pastime. During awake periods (which are much longer now), infants will entertain themselves by producing new sounds and repeating them with some modification. This is vocal play. The game becomes even more entertaining when an adult plays along. Lengthy "conversations" can be held if the adult mimics the baby's sound and then waits for a reply. Vowel sounds (*a, e, i, o,* and *u*) are the baby's favorites at first, but soon consonant sounds will follow.
4. *4 to 8 months.* While babies are experimenting with vocal play, they will also begin to babble. Along with the singular vowel and consonant sounds, repetitive syllables such as *a-la-la* will make up much of the daily dialogue. Most interestingly, babies will babble sounds not generally found in their own language. The English *l* and *r* sounds, for example, are vocalized by Chinese and Japanese infants. Hard-of-hearing infants begin to babble at the same time and in the same way as do infants with normal hearing. The sounds made by the hard-of-hearing babies are the same up to about 6 months of age. After that time the rate of babbling and the number of sounds both decrease.
5. *8 to 12 months.* Babbling begins to sound more and more like true language as babies practice the sounds they hear most often and begin to use intonation. Around 8 months, *da-da* may be pro-

nounced, eliciting great pride in all fathers (although the sound has nothing to do with the word *daddy*). A little later *ma-ma* may be sounded to balance the scale (but this, too, will not really mean *mommy*). Finally, by 10 months babies are likely to use these sounds appropriately to address their parents (or any adult who happens to be in the room). Sounds will now be used as attempted words. *Fla* may mean *flower*. *Ma* may mean *milk*. *Ba* may mean *bottle*. (But don't jump to conclusions. *Ba* can also mean *baby*, *bad*, or *blanket*.) Toward the end of this period, babies learn to string sounds together to make "sentences," and often these sentences carry intonations that express meanings such as fear, surprise, or happiness. Children will ask a question with babbled sounds by raising the pitch near the end of the "sentence," as is usual in the English language.

JUST A PHASE?

The first word usually appears around the same time as the onset of walking. If motor development is appreciably ahead of language, either hearing loss or some other language problem may be suspected. Conversely, if motor development lags behind language development, then a motor delay may be indicated.

6. *1 year.* Babies will continue to babble for quite some time into their second year, but around the first birthday, babies pronounce their first true word. This word identifies a person, event, or object in the immediate environment. The most frequently learned words refer to food and food utensils (cookie, milk, bottle), names of people and pets (Mama, Dada, and the child's own name), and the names of toys (ball, doll). After the first word is learned, others follow, slowly. The average 12-month-old has a vocabulary of about 3 to 8 words, each used as one-word expressions (but remember: the baby *understands* about 20 words).

7. *12 to 18 months.* This is the age of the parrot. Your child will listen carefully and yell out a sound in an attempt to mimic your language. At this age, you'll also see that language and thought development are closely related. As the complexity of thought increases, children can express more linguistically complex ideas. For example, as children learn that objects still exist even when they can't be seen (object permanence), they will mention an object or person not present in the room. As the idea of quantity and number develops, children begin to use plural endings and words such as *two* and *more*. When memory becomes more established, they will refer to past events. As the concept of negation is learned, children's favorite word–*no*–appears and is practiced often.

SCIENCE TO TAKE HOME

Baby talk is not bad for your baby. Although you don't want to mispronounce words by saying something like, "I just wuv my wittle, pwitty baby," the sing-song, high-pitched voice that many mothers naturally use is what babies like best. Studies indicate that high-pitched sounds attract an infant's attention, and melodic intonation keeps that attention longer than normal adult conversational tones. In fact, researchers now suspect that this "infant-directed" speech is preferred over adult speech patterns by babies as young as 2 days old (Adler, 1990).

Parenting to Encourage Language Development

- Talk to your baby about what you're doing. As you prepare a meal or shop for food, explain to your baby exactly what you're doing. Point to the food and say simply, "Apples."
- Acknowledge your baby's attempts to communicate. When he points to an object, give it to him. When he claps his hands, clap yours, too.
- When your baby babbles, babble back. Don't worry about using "correct" language; it's more important to show that you understand she is trying to communicate.
- When your baby "talks" to you, talk back. Then pause, leaving time for him to respond.
- When you say "ball," point to a ball. When you say "Mama," point to the baby's mother.
- Use baby sign language. Gestures like waving bye-bye or blowing a kiss are good ways to encourage communication skills.
- Fill your baby's day with music. Like language, music has changing rhythms, tones, and inflections.

Avoid

- Using vague or general terms. Don't call a rattle a *toy.* Don't call a cookie *food.* Try to be very specific.
- Using pronouns too often. Saying, "I'm going to give you a bath," won't teach the same language lesson as "Mommy's going to give Katie a bath."

- Confusing your baby with intonations that give mixed signals. If you calmly and softly say, "No, don't touch that," your baby won't get the message. Inflection and intonation are both part of language that need to be consistent.

REMEMBER

Language development doesn't begin the day your baby first says a word. It begins right from birth. Throughout their early months, babies are listening and learning constantly. They quickly learn words through repetition, tone of voice, and association, and they will respond to words long before they can actually speak them.

- Being afraid to coo and babble. Mimicking your baby's sounds teaches the interaction of conversation.
- Confusing your baby with full sentences like, "This is a spoon" when teaching new words. Simply point to the spoon and say "spoon" clearly.
- Feeling silly talking to your infant. It's an important step in language development.
- Underestimating your baby's ability to "talk" back even before he or she first says a word. Ask your infant, "Do you want juice or water in your bottle?" and wait for an "answer." Very soon your baby will learn to fill in the moment of silence with a smile, an arm wave, or a squeal.

Family and Peer Relationships

From the moment of birth we look to those around us for physical and emotional support. The family unit is usually the first support group for a newborn. The quality of this support establishes the bonds of attachment that lay the groundwork for all later relationships. Right from infancy, our children learn the value of close relationships, the security they can gain from family routines, and the unavoidable influence of peer pressure.

Building Friendships

Nine-month-old Tad spied his ten-month-old cousin, Lee, across the crowded room. Both babies looked at each other and let out high-pitched squeals of delight. They flapped their arms and threw their bodies forward toward each other with outstretched hands. "Tad and Lee spend a lot of time together," says Tad's mom, Bonnie, "but that was the first time I realized that they had become good friends."

Children as young as 3 months do enjoy the company of other babies. They can now distinguish different faces, voices, and personalities, and will show obvious pleasure at the sight of another baby. Given the opportunity to play with the same child regularly, even infants can become friends. Side-by-side play with other babies gives your child opportunities to get used to being with other children, watching them, and imitating their actions. These are important first steps toward learning how to interact with others.

Building friendships is a slow process that doesn't happen right away for infants, but you can get the ball rolling by setting up play dates for your baby. If you do this, make your young guest (and his or her caregiver, who should not drop off an infant at a play date) feel at ease right from the start by offering a snack–this is always a welcomed ice-breaker because it gives the baby and parent time to slowly take in the environment. Then offer your little guest a choice of a few toys–bring the toys to the guest so he or she doesn't have to stray too far from home base (Mom or Dad's leg). Even if the play date never leaves the parent's lap, don't despair. Continue your efforts to make the guest comfortable. At this age, leaving the lap is the first step in the socialization process.

When you plan a play date, you may envision two babies giggling and playing peacefully with each other, but after the first visit you'll realize that children this young have no claim to social graces–they aren't able to consider another's point of view, and so sharing and cooperative play are out of the question. This doesn't mean you should call off the visits; it means you need to stay vigilant and patient. Children can't learn to play nicely without lots of opportunities to figure out how it's done.

Parenting to Help Children Develop Friendships

- Give your baby opportunities to spend time with other babies.
- Understand that playing side by side with other babies gives your child a chance to watch other children and imitate their actions.
- Invite the parent of your baby's friend to stay for the play date also.
- Stay nearby when your baby plays with a new friend. They are not yet ready to be socially pleasant or secure.

Avoid

- Waiting for your baby to grow up before you arrange play dates.
- Being surprised if your baby's play date never leaves the mother's lap. Give the child time.
- Expecting your baby to be a good friend to other babies. He or she is not yet able to share, interact nicely, or understand group dynamics.
- Giving up playdates because it looks like your baby is not playing anyway. These dates give babies the opportunity to watch, observe, and learn.

Family Rituals and Routines

Eight-month-old Billy doesn't have a bedtime routine. Some nights his mom, Anna, rocks him to sleep; sometimes she puts him in his crib, shuts the door, and lets him cry until he nods off. And sometimes his parents let him run around until he drops. "Every night is different, but it's always a struggle," says Anna. "Are all kids like this?"

Yes. Babies have no idea when or how they should sleep, or eat, or bathe, or do any other daily activity. They need their parents to set down pleasant but nonnegotiable routines to give order and security to their lives. You can introduce daily routines when your baby is as young as 3 or 4 months.

Before 3 months of age, babies may be too immature to follow a regular schedule–they are still settling into life outside the womb. But soon, you'll notice that their crying is more reasonable and predictable. They can go 3 or 4 hours between feedings and have longer periods of alertness between naps. At this time developing routines for activities like bedtime, naptime, and mealtime is not only possible, but necessary. Babies need your help to regulate their inner clocks and to organize their needs and functions. Here's how routines work after the age of 3 months, using sleep time as an example:

Set a definite time for sleep. Taking into consideration your baby's daily schedule and sleep needs, determine a time for naptime and bedtime that coincides with his need for rest and then stick with it.

Create a sleep ritual. Make the time before sleep as routinely tranquil and predictable as possible. Then you might develop a bedtime ritual within that routine. A typical ritual might go something like

---

SCIENCE TO TAKE HOME

Researchers Daniel Kessler and Peter Dawson have found that sustenance, stimulation, and support are important elements that enable young children to thrive. They have reported that for these elements to achieve maximum benefit, they need to be organized into meaningful patterns. They advise: "A child-care system that provides regular routines that are somewhat structured around the child's own biological rhythms promotes better outcomes for the child" (Kessler, Dawson, et al., 1999).

---

this: You carry your baby to the bedroom, turn on a night light, sit to sing a lullaby, kiss a few stuffed animals goodnight, kiss your baby, and lay her in her bed. Say goodnight and leave the room while she is still awake.

Don't expect babies to accept their new routines immediately. They may cry and complain, but stay firm and calm. Persistent repetition will help them understand that this is what happens at this time of day. The sameness of a sleep routine, for example, carries comfort, security, and a promise that the separation caused by sleep is predictable and temporary.

Whatever routines and rituals you create, make sure they're ones you can repeat and can pass on to your child's caregivers. If you build a routine that includes a story, a song, and a nightlight, your babysitter will never get your child to sleep if he or she doesn't follow the same steps (in the same order). These are the signals that tell a baby what to do next.

Babies need to know when they eat, when they nap, and when they play. Routines and rituals that map out a predictable schedule ease the transitions that can otherwise confuse and scare young babies. As they try to figure out how the world they now live in works, routines give them a sense of security and control.

Parenting To Create Rituals and Routines

- After the third month, establish a consistent daily schedule so your child feels in control of her world.
- For a few days, keep track of when your baby seems hungry and tired. Use this information to build a schedule around his biological clock.
- When your baby gets a little older and begins to resist her bedtime, first make sure the scheduled time still fits her biological clock. If

---

CONSIDER

Creating daily routines for your child doesn't mean you have to follow a regimented schedule that cannot be broken. A surprise visit from Grandma is a good time to postpone a nap. You don't have to beg off a fun trip with your spouse because it would interfere with the baby's playtime. Babies can adapt easily to occasional changes without any harm. A consistent daily routine is something you can use to help babies set their biological and emotional clocks, but don't let it take all the fun out of spontaneous activities.

---

it does, use something neutral, like a kitchen timer or a certain song, to signal sleep time. She'll hear the sound and know what to expect next.

Avoid

- Worrying if you occasionally break your baby's routine. No one's life can be completely schedule driven.
- Giving up on the idea of routines because you work and life is hectic enough. Routines make life easier! When your baby learns that he always has a healthy snack while you prepare dinner and that you read him a story after the dishes are done, he won't be whining and crying for those things the minute you walk in the door.
- Creating a bedtime ritual that you won't want to repeat every single night.
- Skipping over a bedtime ritual because you're in a hurry. It will take you much longer in the end to get your child to sleep without it.

Peer Pressure

Nine-month old Tina sat contentedly in her high chair. In one fist she clutched a cookie and in the other her bottle of juice. Tina's 3-year-old brother, Ryan, sat at the kitchen table nearby, drinking his juice from a sippy cup. Tina stared at the cup, then looked back at her bottle. She watched Ryan drink from the cup. She carefully studied how he put the cup to his mouth. And then, *boom!* Tina threw her bottle across the room and grabbed for Ryan's cup. With a quick lunge and a loud cry, she grabbed the cup from his hands.

Although to Tina's mom this looked like an infant tantrum, it may actually have been peer influence in its neophyte form. We know babies are great imitators, but have you thought about what makes them copy

---

REMEMBER

Babies need to know when they eat, when they nap, and when they play. Routines and rituals that map out a predictable schedule ease the transitions that can otherwise confuse and scare young babies. As they try to figure out how the world they now live in works, routines give them a sense of security and control. You can introduce daily routines when your baby is as young as 3 or 4 months.

---

others? They want to do what the people around them do. They want to be like the crowd. They want to fit in. That's what socialization and peer influence is all about. Although peer pressure isn't in full swing at this age, you'll occasionally see glimpses of its development.

Parents, on the other hand, often fall into the hands of full-blown negative peer pressure of their own at this early stage. If little Christy gives up her bottle at 10 months, so should my Allie. If little Keith has the latest toy, so will my Susie. If little Clark is walking, so should my Jacquline be. If you don't want your child to think he has to do what everybody else does when he's 14, watch out how you, yourself, buckle to peer pressure now.

Your baby's development is unique and individual. All the timelines in all the parenting books are only guidelines based on averages. If you have any concerns about developmental delays, talk to your baby's doctor or pediatric developmental specialist. Unless there is a diagnosed problem, you shouldn't spend any time trying to keep up with the Joneses' kid. Be cautious about letting peer pressure creep into your parenting style or you'll soon find that the little name-brand shoes you now buy become the way your child learns to identify herself among her peers as she grows through childhood.

Parenting to Help Children Deal with Peer Pressure

- Be aware that peer pressure isn't necessarily a bad thing. Trying to be like everybody else pushes your baby to try new things.
- Watch for signs of peer influence–especially from siblings.
- Let your baby grow on his own clock without worrying if his progress is as good as other babies'.

REMEMBER

Babies are great imitators. They want to do what the people around them do. They want to be like the crowd. They want to fit in. That's what socialization and peer influence is all about. Although peer pressure isn't in full swing at this age, you'll occasionally see glimpses of its development.

Avoid

- Giving in to the negative side of peer pressure by comparing your baby to others–she is like no other!
- Being too concerned that other babies have more things than your baby. Your love and attention are the most valuable gifts you can give a child.
- Teaching your baby that being like other babies is very important. It is not necessary to wear the same kind of clothes, or go to the same baby classes, or have the same toys.

Personal Growth

Inside your baby is a unique individual who will grow to think and feel things that no other person on the face of the earth has ever thought or felt before. This process of personal growth is influenced daily through each experience of success, failure, satisfaction, and frustration. Each social interaction teaches your child more about who he or she is and who he or she will become. Three aspects of personal growth that you will find particularly interesting to watch are the development of a sense of self, the growth of independence through autonomy, and the evolvement of responsibility.

Sense of Self

Although it's hard to imagine, your baby has no idea that you and he or she are not one and the same person. In fact, babies have no way of knowing that any other people exist separately from themselves at all. A sense of self as a separate body and mind, distinct from others, does not develop until the child is about 18 months old. Much of life before this time is devoted to learning to make this distinction.

Sense of Body

The first step in becoming aware of the self as a separate distinct individual is the realization that the body is separate and unique from all other bodies. During the first 18 months, children gradually become aware of their bodies' boundaries and wholeness. They learn that they are a nonfragmented, physical whole. Children as young as 18 weeks will gaze at their image in a mirror, but they don't recognize that they are seeing a reflection of themselves until sometime in the second year of life. By 18 months, children will point to pictures of themselves when their names are called. It is not surprising that the development of object permanence is related to the development of self-recognition. The development of an understanding of the continued permanence and existence and continuity of the self is the critical first step in the formation of self-identity.

Because the baby's earliest sense of self has to do with the body, it is logical that parental reaction to a physical activity or to body parts forms the basis of the child's perception that the physical self and the pleasure derived from it are good or bad. If, for example, the mother observes the baby exploring parts of the body, including the genitals, she will bolster his feelings about himself if she allows the exploration to continue. If a child gets the impression that her parents disapprove of something about her body, her overall sense of self can be negatively affected in the long run.

It is the parent's job during this period to have a positive attitude toward the child's discovery of the body and to encourage the child to feel, explore, and examine every finger, toe, and knee. You can encourage this growing sense of self by using words to reflect a positive image of the child's body. Say things such as "What strong fingers you have" and "You are so beautiful."

Self as a Doer

Slowly, during the first year, babies become aware of themselves as someone who has power to make things happen. They learn that they can summon someone's attention by calling out; they learn they can grab an object and throw it aside. They learn they can make a noise happen by shaking a rattle. It is thrilling for a baby to learn this lesson. Pulling a page from a magazine shows the power of action to make a change. The baby will tear page after page, marveling in this ability to produce an effect.

To encourage the baby's sense of self as someone who can make things happen, talk to your baby about her accomplishments. Say, "Oh, you've found your toes!" "You made that spoon fall." "You make me laugh."

Male or Female Self

At 12 months a child's awakening sense of gender can be seen. A 1-year-old girl who is shown a film involving people of both sexes will look longer at the females than at the males. This indicates that the baby has the first inkling of gender identity. At 18 months, babies will notice that boys and girls have different sexual organs.

You can encourage the development of gender identity by using the words *boy* or *girl* when you address your baby. Statements like "What a happy girl you are" or "You are a good boy" help your baby's early identification with the words that define his or her gender.

Parenting to Help Children Develop a Sense of Self

- Admire your baby–simply for existing. Every time you smile and tell your baby she is beautiful, she is given a piece of information that she will use to learn she is a separate and valued individual.
- Praise your baby's accomplishments. When you reward your baby's smile with a smile of your own, or when you applaud his ability to roll, kick, or make noises, you fuel the infant's development of a sense of value and associated self-esteem. Infants take pleasure in feeling that their actions can produce a joyful response from their parents.
- Be attentive to your baby's innate needs, emotions, temperamental characteristics, and cognitive competencies. This attention helps an infant have a dawning awareness that she is important and loved. She learns that her needs are met by the actions of others who can be trusted.
- You can influence the way your baby learns about his separate body by the way you handle his skin. Massage it, rub it, feel it. The sen-

---

SCIENCE TO TAKE HOME

The development of self has been studied by presenting a mirror to infants and noting how they respond. One of the earliest studies to use this technique was published by Dixon (1957), who longitudinally observed five infants from the ages of 4 to 12 months. He found a four-stage developmental sequence of visual self-recognition:

1. **The baby has no interest in the reflection in the mirror.**
2. **The baby responds to the image in the mirror as if it were an interesting playmate.**
3. **The baby is able to differentiate between his or her own reflection and the mirror image of another child.**
4. **The baby shows definite signs of self-recognition.**

---

sations and perceptions this causes help an infant construct a mental picture of his body boundaries.

- Encourage the concept of object permanence by hiding a toy under a blanket and then showing your baby that when you remove the blanket the toy is still there.
- Talk to your baby about her accomplishments. Say things such as "You clapped your hands and made a sound" or "You kicked your feet and make the toy fall down."
- Encourage the development of gender identity by using the words *boy* or *girl* when you address your baby.

REMEMBER

Your little baby has no idea that you and he or she are not one and the same person. In fact, babies have no way of knowing that any other people exist separately from themselves at all. A sense of self as a separate body and mind, distinct from others, does not develop until the child is about 18 months old. Much of life before this time is devoted to learning to make this distinction.

Avoid

- Stopping your baby's body explorations. Don't get upset if he touches his genitals. Don't keep pulling his hands away from his face or ears. Let his fingers explore this fascinating thing called a body.
- Assuming your baby's motives are the same as those of an older child. She doesn't rip up magazines for destructive purposes; she does it to see what happens when she grabs hold and pulls.
- Worrying that telling your baby she is a "good little girl" is a sexist remark. Political correctness is not an issue when you're teaching your baby gender identity.
- Being embarrassed by the fact that you think your baby is the most fabulous human being on the face of the earth. This attitude will help her develop a positive self-image.

Autonomy

"It's obvious that Katie has a mind of her own," laughs her mom, Sarah. "No matter how many times I tell her not to, she loves to drop her spoon on the floor and cry until I give it back to her. I think she just likes to see me bend over a hundred times a day!"

Before they can even talk, babies like Katie take tiny steps toward autonomy. Autonomy is the need to be independent—to act on one's own, to think for oneself. It is a force that pushes even infants to find ways to control their world. It is the reason for the push and pull between dependence and independence that parents and children struggle with throughout the years of childhood.

Using their physical vocabulary, babies will slowly learn that for each action there is a reaction. Without anyone's help they can grab at Mom's earrings and make her cry out. They can drop things on the floor and make others pick them up. They can laugh out loud and make people smile. What power!

To further develop this sense of independence, babies need some time alone. This means you don't need to constantly entertain your child. Leave her alone for a while each day to play, to daydream, and to amuse herself. These private moments are important to the baby's ability to develop a sense of self that's separate from her parents. They offer a baby the opportunity to use her senses to take in all the sounds and smells and sights of her environment. These quiet moments allow her to build a picture of how she relates to the rest of the world.

You can also encourage autonomy by letting your baby fall asleep without your help. If you always rock, feed, or soothe him to sleep, you take away his natural ability to self-soothe and therefore cause him to be more dependent on you. Many parents unknowingly teach their babies to associate their presence (while rocking, feeding, or back patting) with falling asleep. If the parent is then not able or willing to always supply this sleep environment, the baby cannot sleep and will cry throughout the night. "Putting" a baby to sleep teaches him that he cannot survive separation from Mom and Dad. It teaches him to rely on others to supply the transitional environment between wakefulness and sleep. All babies over the age of 6 months can fall asleep without the help of their parents—if their parents give them the opportunity to learn how by not picking them up every time they cry.

Crying is a baby's way of controlling the level of stimulation; the cry helps to discharge tension and fatigue and allows the baby to fall asleep. As a bonus, this skill of self-comforting nurtures the child's

---

CONSIDER

If you bring your face very close to your baby's face, you may be invading the baby's private space. This will cause a baby to avert the eyes, turn the head away, and even cry. This is usually more of a problem with relatives and friends than with parents whom the baby trusts. Encourage siblings, family, and friends to respect the baby's personal space and keep a bit of distance between them.

---

sense of control over his world and promotes a necessary sense of independence. After the age of 6 months, let your baby cry for about 10 minutes to lull himself to sleep. The crying won't hurt him, and the experience will nurture his sense of autonomy.

Your baby's personality will in many ways dictate how and when she decides to act independently. Some children are very outgoing and have no fear of moving away from Mom and Dad (directly into the street if you're not careful). Others are more hesitant and need more time to break away from your leg and join the crowd. If your baby clings to you in new situations, don't pressure her to be "brave" by pushing her away. You'll lengthen the state of dependency if you force her to try something she is not ready for. Give opportunities for separation and exploration, and then wait until your child feels comfortable enough to reach out and explore them.

Parenting to Nurture Autonomy

- Accept your baby's "seek-and-destroy" behavior as exploratory adventures rather than destructive acts.
- Respect your baby's ability to self-soothe by letting him occasionally cry himself to sleep.
- Give your baby some time to be alone each day.
- Let your baby learn how to entertain and soothe herself.
- After 6 months of age, give your baby space to learn that he is an individual separate from you.
- Respect your baby's personality by giving her plenty of room and time to develop a sense of independence.

REMEMBER

Autonomy is the need to be independent—to act on one's own, to think for oneself. It is a force that pushes even infants to find ways to control their own world. It is the reason for the push and pull between dependence and independence that parents and children struggle with throughout the years of childhood.

Avoid

- Ignoring your baby's cries if they are signaling physical distress, hunger or pain.
- Invading your baby's privacy by continually putting your face extremely close to his if he indicates that he doesn't like it.
- Always rocking your baby to sleep or feeding him as he falls off to sleep. This will prevent him from learning how to self-soothe.

- Clinging to your baby, inhibiting the natural separation that must occur in order for the child to gain a sense of autonomy. When she crawls away from you, smile and applaud; don't rush to the rescue and keep her from exploring.
- Thinking that you must interact with your baby constantly. To "find" themselves, babies need some time alone. Time spent quietly observing and moving helps infants learn that they have a separate body that produces separate behaviors.

Responsibility

Responsibility means being trustworthy, reliable, and accountable. It means being able to answer for one's conduct. Of course these are traits we all want to see in our children, but they are not inborn–they are learned. Be assured that initially infants feel no sense of responsibility toward anyone. Not to you, not to a sibling, not to a friend, not to Grandma, not even toward themselves. They are completely unaccountable for their behavior. However, this is the time when the seeds of responsibility are planted.

We all get our first lessons in responsibility by observing the kind of care and treatment given to us by the adults around us. Responsible adults take care of an infant's need for food, affection, and physical comfort as quickly as possible. They don't let babies scream themselves into a fit to teach them who's in charge. They give lots of unconditional love. They teach children to be responsible by being responsible toward them.

The next step in teaching responsibility to a baby focuses on the age-old method of assigning chores. Of course you cannot hold your infant responsible for cleaning up the mashed peas she spits all over the wall, but she can learn at this early age that cleaning up is a part of life. Don't clean up after your baby only when you've put him down for a nap. Let him watch you clean up with a song and a smile every day. Teach her by your own example that putting toys away naturally follows the act of playing with them. Show him that cleaning up a spill is not a punishment; it's simply the responsible thing to do. As your baby moves into his or her second year, he or she can move from watching you clean up to helping you. Make a game of picking up toys and dropping them in their container. Guide your baby's hand to pick up and clean up. Older children resist chores only when they have learned that it's not their job to be responsible for their things.

Parenting to Teach Responsibility

- Respond to your baby's cries of hunger and pain to show her what it means to be a responsible person.
- Let your infant see you clean up his mess and his toys with a smile.
- Ask your 1-year-old to help you pick up toys every day.

Avoid

- Expecting a baby between birth and 18 months to feel a sense of responsibility toward anyone.
- Trying to build a sense of responsibility by making an infant wait for food or comfort. The very opposite lesson is learned.
- Teaching your baby that chores are a negative thing by complaining about the cleanup every time she makes a mess.
- Always cleaning up when your baby is out of sight. Let him see how it works.
- Underestimating your 1-year-old's ability to help you clean up. With a little encouragement, she can be a big help.

REMEMBER

Infants feel no sense of responsibility toward anyone. However, this is the time when the seeds of responsibility are planted.

Character Formation

What kind of character traits do you wish for your child? When you think about this question you'll find your mind considering your own values and morals. You'll picture a person who is self-disciplined and in control of impulsive behavior. And you'll imagine someone who has respect for others. These are the building blocks of character that none of us are born with. We learn them from the world we live in. As their first teachers, your example is the foundation on which your children will build the sense of morality, values, personal discipline, and social manners that will form their character.

Values and Morals

To adopt values such as honesty and kindness and to develop a moral sense of right and wrong, we all need to be able to experience emotions that are associated with the consequences of one's conduct–emotions such as anxiety, guilt, remorse, and discomfort. Each of these emotional underpinnings of conscience begins to emerge slowly after the first birthday. But before this time, babies' lack of identity separate from others makes it impossible for them to feel emotions connected to the well-being of others.

But this doesn't mean that values and morality are not a consideration during infancy. In fact, the lessons that lead a child to adopt cultural values and morals begin very early in life. From birth to 18 months, you teach your baby many lessons about right and wrong by the way you treat him or her.

Your daily interactions with your baby set the stage for the development of values and morals that match your own. Infants who are cuddled, loved, and cared for and whose emotional needs are consistently met are likely to demonstrate caring behavior themselves when they are older. By contrast, toddlers whose emotional needs have been ignored tend to hit others and ignore their distress. This is a logical consequence: The more often infants participate in loving and fun activities with their parents, the more opportunities there are for observational learning about family and cultural standards and for the transmission of expectations.

Feeling loved has a profound and enduring effect on a person's feelings for others—this is the core of morality. Showing love and affection to children teaches them to care about others and to respond with kindness and empathy to others in distress. Simply put: We learn to care about others by being cared for. This is how babies learn about the morals and values of their family and culture.

Parenting to Teach Values and Morals

- Show your baby that his actions can cause good and bad feelings in others.
- Say the word *ouch* whenever she hurts herself; then say *ouch* again whenever she hurts someone else.
- Let your child know that you take pleasure in his existence. Answer his calls for help as soon as possible.
- When your child is too rough with pets or other children, teach her the word and action of *gentle*. If she pulls the dog's fur, take her hand away, firmly say no, and then rub her hand gently over the fur, saying with a smile, "Gentle."
- Communicate your love for your child right from the start. Children who feel good about their relationship with their parents want to adopt behaviors that please them.

REMEMBER

Children adopt values such as honesty and kindness and develop a moral sense of right and wrong by imitating what they see in the world around them.

Avoid

- Expecting your baby to understand how his actions make others feel. He does not know that pulling his sister's hair hurts her.
- Making your baby scream frantically before you move in to help. This teaches her that people respond to other's distress only after they are pushed to the brink.
- Thinking you can wait until your baby grows up to teach lessons in morals and values. Every smile and frown you give your baby teaches him your standards of good and bad.

Self-Control and Discipline

Infants have no sense of self-control, and no amount of discipline will make them feel accountable for their behavior. This doesn't mean, however, that you shouldn't introduce the idea of discipline to control negative or dangerous impulses. Babies can be taught the concept of self-control–to a point.

CONSIDER

Do not yell, shake, spank, or use long explanations to discipline an infant.

The loudest debate in infant discipline often centers on the right and wrong ways of disciplining a crying baby. Will you spoil a baby by picking her up every time she cries? The answer is: It depends on the age and the reason for the crying. You should promptly pick up a crying infant under 3 months of age. At this stage, the only lesson a crying baby learns when his cries are ignored is that the adults in his world cannot be trusted to take care of him. So put disciplining concerns completely aside for the first 3 months.

After three months, you will begin to discern your baby's hunger and pain cries (which still need to be answered promptly) from her "I'm bored" cries. It's okay to let her cry for 2 or 3 minutes if you're busy with something else. Gradually, your baby will learn that there are times when you can't do exactly what she wants the moment she wants it. She will learn how to soothe and entertain herself sometimes by simply sucking on her fingers, watching her mobile, or cooing and gurgling.

The waiting periods can be extended as your child grows. When your 8-month-old starts to show signs of hunger, don't always sprint for the bottle; sometimes hold him and soothe him with words for a few minutes. When your 10-month-old wants a toy from the top shelf while you're cooking, say, "I know what you want, but I'm busy now. You'll have to wait." Your baby won't want to wait; he'll still pester you, but he's learning that sometimes other people's needs come before his own. To develop self-control, babies need to gradually understand that the world does not revolve around them. The ability to tolerate frustration is an important developmental task for children.

SCIENCE TO TAKE HOME

Infants who do not learn to regulate their frustration reactions tend to be more noncompliant as toddlers (Stifter, Spinard, & Baungart, 1999).

By the time your baby is 7 to 8 months old, he's ready to be told "No" when he behaves inappropriately. Babies under this age have a limited memory and won't recall that a particular action prompted your disapproval. But after 7 months, most babies can make the connection between something they have done and the word *no*. They begin to recognize the sound of the word and associate it with a stern look from their parents. Because babies don't like their parents to look or sound unhappy, this effectively teaches them what they are not allowed to do.

At first this may be confusing for both of you because the actions of babies are not rooted in the kind of motives that drive older children and even adults. When a baby hits another person, for example, it is not for the purpose of hurting that person. Usually it's simply because she's learning about that fascinating law of motion that says for each action there is a reaction. This reflects her growing awareness that she can have an impact on her environment–a healthy realization. Still, it's time to teach her that hitting is not allowed. If your baby hits the dog, for example, say "No" and frown; then take the baby's hand and rub it softly against the dog's fur and smile. Then distract her with a new activity. When she hits the dog again, respond in exactly the same way.

If after repeatedly using this first method of discipline your baby still does not understand that something is not allowed, you can use a discipline approach that is a bit more forceful. The next time she hits the dog, for example, pick her up and move her to another room. Sit down and hold her (facing you) by her shoulders and upper arms. Don't squeeze, but hold her firmly enough so she can't move or squirm away from you. After a minute or two of being held firmly, she will start to show that she doesn't like what's happening. At this point, hold her for another 15 seconds and say, "We're going back to the other room and you can play now, but if you hit the dog again I'm going to have to hold you again." Your baby won't understand all the words, but she'll get the message. If you consistently use this approach the undesirable behavior will stop within 7 to 10 days.

CONSIDER

The trick during these early lessons in discipline is to make sure your baby doesn't get the message that he or she is bad. When your baby pulls your hair, be sure you don't cut emotional ties by putting the baby down and leaving him or her alone. After you say no and put your baby down, calmly draw his or her attention to another activity. This says, "I don't like what you did, but I still love you."

By being consistently firm but not overly reactive, you accomplish two things: You let your child know that the behavior is not allowed, and you reinforce your position as teacher and helper without becoming a hostile opponent. At some point during the second year, babies have enough stored memories like these to help them understand that there are rules that govern the way people treat one another.

Be selective about when you say no. If you overuse it, it loses its punch. Reserve your *no*s for dangerous or harmful situations like when your baby grabs hold of the lamp's electrical cord or bites another child. Try not to say no when your child does something annoying, but essentially harmless. Throwing toys out of the crib, for example, is simply a game, not a dangerous situation.

If you use the word *no* firmly and consistently only when danger looms, by the end of the first year, your baby will begin to realize that you have standards that dictate what she can and cannot do. Knowing this, she will begin to look to you for cues to help her make decisions about her behavior. A toddler crawling toward the open door, for example, will constantly look back to his mother for a cue that will tell him if this is a good idea–if this is "good or bad." The baby is comparing a contemplated action with a parent's standard of right and wrong. This kind of social referencing sets the stage for the development of self-control that is based on parental expectations.

Parenting to Teach Self-Control

- Put disciplining concerns completely aside for the first 3 months.
- Under the age of 3 months, show your infant that she can count on you to answer her cries.
- After 3 months, help your baby learn self-control by letting him occasionally wait a short while for your attention when he cries out of boredom
- Begin to teach your baby the word *no* when she is 7 to 8 months old.

SCIENCE TO TAKE HOME

Do you and your spouse give your baby conflicting emotional cues? The consequences of inconsistency can make it difficult for a child to know what's right and what's wrong. In a study conducted with 1-year-olds, parents were coached to give consistent or conflicting emotional signals when the child was about to explore an unusual toy. The infants adapted much more easily to consistent emotional signals—either both parents happy or both parents fearful—than to conflicting signals. In fact, when they were given conflicting facial responses—happy from the mother and fear from the father, for example—the infants expressed their confusion in a wide range of anxious behaviors. Some sucked their thumbs or rocked in an agitated way; others avoided the situation altogether; still others wandered aimlessly or seemed disoriented. It seems that 1-year-olds are remarkably sensitive to emotional signals from parents (Craig, 1996).

- Use discipline to teach, not to punish.
- When your baby does something he is not allowed to do, follow the two-step discipline plan: (1) Firmly say no with a frown, and (2) distract him with another activity.
- Reserve your *no*s for dangerous or harmful situations.
- Give your baby consistent cues about what is right and wrong.

Avoid

- Expecting a baby between birth and 18 months to have a sense of self-control.
- Worrying that attending to a crying baby under 3 months of age will spoil her.
- Expecting a baby under 7 months to remember what he is and is not allowed to do.
- Overreacting with anger when your baby does something "bad." At this age, babies have no concept of good and bad.
- Implying that the baby is bad. Focus on the undesirable action, not on the child.
- Overusing the word *no*.
- Confusing your baby's developing sense of right and wrong by being inconsistent in your discipline efforts.

REMEMBER

Infants have no sense of self-control, and no amount of discipline will make them feel accountable for their behavior. This doesn't mean, however, that you shouldn't introduce the idea of discipline to control negative or dangerous impulses. Babies can be taught the concept of self-control—to a point. Early training will lay the foundation for effective discipline in later years.

Manners

Thirteen-month-old Kirsten toddled over to her playmate and grabbed the ball right out of her hands. Kirsten's mother scolded, "No. No. You have to share!"

While putting the needs of others first certainly is a sign of good manners, babies aren't ready to do this yet because they don't possess the three things that are necessary to treat other people with consideration: (1) an awareness that they are individuals separate from others, (2) an understanding that their behavior has an impact on other people, and (3) a grasp of the idea that they are capable of controlling their own behavior. Or, to put it in its simplest terms: From birth to 18

AGE DIFFERENCES

Infants learn about politeness by passively watching you. But as soon as your baby begins to talk, you can take advantage of babies' natural love of mimicry to encourage him or her to imitate what you say and do. At this time, your baby still won't appreciate the need and value of manners, but he or she will be thrilled to try words like *thank you* and *please.*

months, babies are naturally egocentric and impulsive. For this reason, they can't share; they can't be quiet in church or temple. They can't let others go first or understand that interrupting a conversation is rude.

Although babies cannot yet understand the concept of politeness, they are always aware and learning about their world from your example–it's never too early to model proper social etiquette. Right from infancy, you should treat your child politely. Use a pleasant voice and a smile when you say hello. Stay attuned to your baby's nonverbal cues; responding to cries of boredom, for example, shows respect for your baby's thoughts and feelings. When your baby holds out a piece of food or a toy to share with you, say "Thank you." When your baby shows appreciation with a smile, be sure to say, "You're welcome!" These models of polite behavior build a baby's sense of self-respect and they get the child ready to respect others. Infants who are treated courteously grow up feeling emotionally secure enough to deal positively and constructively with the people around them.

SCIENCE TO TAKE HOME

A poll conducted by *U.S. News & World Report* found that 9 out of 10 Americans think incivility is a serious problem, and nearly half think it is extremely serious. Seventy-eight percent say the problem has worsened in the past 10 years (Marks, 1996).

Parenting to Teach Good Manners

- Create social play opportunities where your baby can begin to learn how to socialize.
- Expect your baby to be egocentric and impulsive.
- Treat your baby politely. Say "Please" and "Thank you." Your example is your best teaching tool.
- Be polite to your baby by responding quickly to his cries of hunger or discomfort. This will teach him how to deal positively with other people.

CONSIDER

Prayers of thanks for family, home, health, and daily bread teach children to express gratitude rather than taking things for granted.

REMEMBER

From birth to 18 months, babies are naturally egocentric and impulsive. For this reason, they can't share; they can't be quiet in church or temple. They can't let others go first or understand that interrupting a conversation is rude.

Avoid

- Expecting your baby to share. It's just not going to happen.
- Thinking it's not necessary to use good manners around your baby. Your actions dictate the kind of social attitude she will use herself as she grows.
- Underestimating your baby's ability to be socially polite. Teach him to wave bye-bye and to say "Hi."
- Waiting for your baby to grow up before thinking about teaching good manners. Many lessons can be learned in babyhood.

18 to 36 Months

STAGE 2

Dear Diary,

Whew! As Christopher turns 3 tomorrow, I get dizzy just thinking about the past year and a half. This was one little boy who jumped into the "terrible twos" with both feet running. It seemed like overnight he became a bundle of unstoppable energy. In this short time he's learned to climb up and down stairs, run with lightning speed, scale new heights, and poke into all kinds of places. I learned quickly that since I can't slow him down, it's best to batten down the hatches so he can run and explore in a safety-proofed area. I've put corner guards on the sharp-edged table corners, safety locks on cabinet doors and drawers, and gates across staircases. Now he can explore without driving me crazy with worry.

Emotionally, Christopher has changed a great deal. He went through a phase where he couldn't decide if he wanted to smother me with hugs and kisses or run away and hide if I tried to hold him on my lap. One minute he loved me, the next he'd be hitting me and pushing me away. I've read that this is a child's way of learning how to be his own person, separate from his parents, but I have to admit there were times when it bothered me to be pushed aside like that.

I guess what bothered me most during that time was Christopher's temper tantrums. They were so unpredictable–one minute he'd be happily playing with a toy and the next he'd throw it across the room and dissolve into a fit of anger. I'm glad that phase is almost over. He seems to be able to do more now and to talk about his feelings, which has cut down on those explosive outbursts. I'm also glad that he's also getting over his fear of large dogs and loud noises. For a long time, there was just no way I could convince him that there was no need to get so frightened. I guess it just takes time and experience to learn what's dangerous and what's not.

It looks like Christopher is going to be the brains of the family–he's so smart! His memory seems to be much better than it used to be, and I can see that that helps him figure things out by himself (or at least try until he gets frustrated and screams for help). He's also talking a blue streak now. Every day I'm surprised by some new sentence (or paragraph!) that he comes out with. I especially enjoy watching Christopher's imagination in action. I just love to watch when he plays with his stuffed animals and pretends to be the mommy and gives them big hugs and kisses. He also plays with his friends much better now than he did a few months ago. Now he is able to share and interact with other children, and he really likes to get together with other children.

I'm always surprised that he knows exactly when we're supposed to go places. It's like he has a clock in his head–and heaven forbid if the schedule changes. Christopher likes everything to be on schedule, and he wants to do things today just like we did them yesterday. In fact, I can't even get him to go to bed if I don't read the same story and kiss all his stuffed animals in the same order every night.

One thing is for sure: Christopher certainly has a mind of his own. He is very big on the words me *and* mine. *He tells me several times every day, "Me do it." He has strong opinions about what he wants to wear, what he wants to eat, when he wants to sleep, and even what TV shows he wants to watch. He is definitely becoming his own little person with thoughts, desires, and needs that are uniquely his own. Thankfully, he's slowly becoming less self-centered. Now he is more willing (and able) to do a few chores around the house–he can sweep the floor with the child broom I bought him; he can clean up his toys (sometimes); and he can help clean up the spills and messes he makes with his food. I think he actually likes helping me. It makes him feel important and needed.*

The last few months have been a time for learning a lot about how the world is divided into "right" and "wrong." Christopher is getting the idea that there are certain things he can't do; that we have rules; that there are consequences when he breaks the rules. This has made life a little harder and yet a little easier on him. It's hard for him to remember all the things he can and can't do, but the rules also seem to give him boundaries that keep him from feeling overwhelmed and unsure about what to expect from me. He knows I will be happy when he does something he knows is good, and he knows I will be unhappy when he misbehaves. There's so much to learn for such a little person. Then it all comes together and seems worthwhile when out of the blue he looks at me and says, "I love you Mommy."

Emotional Health

In this second stage from 18 to 36 months, the emotional life of a child is very much like a roller coaster ride. The highs are very high, and the lows are frighteningly low. These children are experiencing the thrill and the danger of moving away from their parents. They want to be separate, but they don't want to be alone. They want to do everything for themselves, but they don't always know how. They want to be "big," but they also want to be cuddled. It's a difficult but exciting time to be alive.

Love and Affection

The task of making your child feel secure in your love and affection continues even as your "baby" now pushes away from you looking for some independence. She may become less affectionate and more adventurous. She doesn't always want to cuddle, and when she's had enough, she arches her back to slide off your lap. There may be days when she doesn't even want you to touch her chair. She has just learned that she is a person separate from you, and she's now spending much of her time testing these boundaries. Still, she needs your unconditional love.

Two-year-old Bonnie was at her cousin's birthday party and feeling daring. She moved a few feet away from her mother's leg, then a few feet more. When she turned back and didn't immediately see her mom, she panicked. "At first she wants nothing to do with me, and then she gets so upset when she can't see me," says her mom. "I don't know what she wants anymore." If your baby is in Stage 2 between 18 and 36 months, you've certainly noticed this push and pull between wanting to be with you and wanting to be away from you. He wants to do things for himself. He wants to be "big" like older siblings or friends. But a toddler's emotional need to be independent and at the same time feel secure in your love and presence can cause some difficult days.

SCIENCE TO TAKE HOME

Byron Egeland and Alan Sroufe of the University of Minnesota have studied the importance of early mother–child relationships. They found that children who had not received sensitive, responsive care in the first few years of life were at significantly higher risk for a wide range of poor developmental outcomes. For example, children who had received less sensitive care were vulnerable in the following ways:

- **They had more difficulty forming relationships with peers in preschool and early adolescence.**
- **They had lower levels of school achievement, especially in adolescence.**
- **They were more likely to require special education (72 percent in special education by third grade).**
- **They exhibited more behavioral problems.**
- **They were more likely to use drugs and alcohol during adolescence.**

However, children who had an early history of secure relationships were less vulnerable to environmental threats than those who had poorer early relationships (Hawley, 1998a).

CONSIDER

In some cases, parents have a particular difficulty providing sensitive care to their children because of their own early experiences in life. Research has shown that parents who remember their own parents as cold and unresponsive are likely to act the same way with their children (Main & Goldwyn, 1984).

(See the following section, "Joy and Anger.") Ironically, when your toddler is most emotionally confused and difficult to handle, that's when he or she most needs love and attention that is consistent, calm, and unconditional.

It's not always easy to give unconditional love and affection to a child between 18 and 36 months. Their love-you/hate-you attitude can easily cause you to withdraw your own affection. For example, if your child refuses your kiss and runs away, it's tempting to teach him a lesson by withholding your affection when he returns a moment later and demands a kiss. You may also find yourself simply too worn out from chasing your toddler around to constantly give him the love he craves.

Whatever the reason, withholding love from a child this age can make the situation even worse. If a parent is unable or unwilling to give a child a consistent sense of love and security, the child may decide to use a tactic sometimes called *love by irritation.* The need for your love and attention is so strong right now, that your toddler will do anything to have it. If the only way to get your attention is to act up—that's what he'll do. The second he hits you and yells "I hate you," he's guaranteed to have your full attention. It works every time. In a study of temper tantrums, researchers presented a case of a child prone to tantrums in which parental attempts to ignore or discipline with a time-out procedure were unsuccessful in stopping the behavior. When it was discovered that the child received almost no personal attention from the parents, except during tantrums, the parents were instructed to each give the child five minutes of individual, positive attention per day. This simple offering of love and affection was successful in eliminating the problem behavior and improving the child's level of happiness (Thelen, 1979).

This is further evidence that children feel our affection the most when they have our undivided attention. Each child needs us to take time every day when we can give personal, one-on-one time to make the child feel special. About 20 minutes a day of quality time devoted to mutually enjoyable activities will play a significant role in keeping the parent–child relationship close.

You can avoid many of the "terrible twos" problems if you understand this emotional confusion that your child lives with. Most of this need–reject syndrome is caused by a struggle inside your child—not a struggle against you. You can secure the bonds of love and affection by giving your child the freedom to move away, knowing that he or she can always return to your open arms.

Parenting to Nurture Love and Affection

- Allow your toddler to push you away, and welcome her when she returns.
- Give unconditional love even when it seems your toddler doesn't want it.

AGE DIFFERENCES

This struggle between dependence and independence occurs in two primary stages of child development—first between the ages of 18 and 36 months, and then again in the early teen years. As you deal with your toddler's push and pull between wanting to please you and wanting to defy you (and the temper tantrums that go with it), keep in mind that this is good practice for when it happens again a few years down the road!

- Accept the push and pull between wanting to be with you and wanting to be away from you.
    - Give love and attention that is consistent, calm, and unconditional.
    - Give personal, one-on-one time to your child each day.

REMEMBER

Most of this need–reject syndrome is caused by a struggle inside your child–not a struggle against you. You can secure the bonds of love and affection by giving your child the freedom to move away, knowing that he or she can always return to your open arms.

Avoid

- Withdrawing your own affection when your toddler pushes you away or refuses a kiss.
- Passing on the legacy of "cold" parenting if your own parents withheld unconditional love.
- Letting your child seek love by irritation. Give him positive attention when he is being good.

Joy and Anger

Between the ages of 18 and 36 months, you will see the most delightful displays of pure, spontaneous joy you will ever see in your child. These children have no hesitation about showing positive feelings. They jump up and down, clap their hands, and squeal with happiness. This is a wonderful time for laughing and rolling on the floor with glee with your children. Unfortunately, it won't last long. During the course of preschool socialization, most children learn to control unrestrained emotional expression. Spontaneous, open expressiveness becomes embarrassing and is considered babyish. So enjoy it now while you can.

In the same way that these children have no qualms about showing spontaneous joy, they have no hesitation about expressing their anger–no matter where they are or who they're with. Twenty-six-month-old Denny sat fidgeting in the supermarket cart. Soon he was screaming and headbanging. "I wanna go!" he yelled. "I wanna go!" Denny didn't care that his mother was embarrassed because he was creating a scene–Denny and all other children his age see the world only from their own viewpoint and are very quick to anger when the world doesn't go their way. This is the age of the "terrible twos" and tantrums. Get ready.

Tantrums are the result of frustration–frustration at the inability to master a task, to communicate a desire, or to understand why things are as they are. It's like blowing an emotional fuse. In fact, an intense tantrum can frighten a child (even more than it frightens you), making the child feel overwhelmed and even more helpless than before.

Because they can't verbalize the intense emotions they feel, these children need a way to vent the anger they feel when frustrated. Temper tantrums are the answer. Actually, this ability to direct their anger toward the source of frustration (very often you) is a sign of healthy development. Knowing what's causing frustration is the first step toward learning how to remedy it.

SCIENCE TO TAKE HOME

When 159 firstborn infants were studied at 18 months of age, temper tantrums 2 to 3 times per week were the norm. No association was found between sleeping problems and temper tantrums, and their incidence was not related to the child's developmental status or social class (Ounsted & Simons, 1978).

You can help your child understand the emotion of anger through your own example. When your toddler rips up your favorite book, she needs to see that it makes you angry. You shouldn't hide your feelings or, on the other hand, lash out in an explosive rage. Through your example, your child will learn how to acknowledge anger and deal with it without throwing a tantrum. You might say, "I'm so angry with you for destroying my book. I don't even want to be with you right now so I'm going to leave and come back when I've calmed down."

You can also teach your child about intensity levels of anger. By using different words to describe the intensity of angry feelings (e.g., annoyed, aggravated, irritated, frustrated, angry, furious, and enraged) children as young as 2½ can learn to understand that anger is a complex emotion with different levels of energy. For example, you might say, "I was so *annoyed* when I couldn't find my car keys," or "That person must have been *furious* when the kids put spray paint on his car."

CONSIDER

Very few of us were taught how to recognize and understand our own anger as a fact of life during childhood. Many of us were punished for showing anger, and we were often made to feel guilty for even feeling it. So now we may try to repress it in our children or deny it when we see it. Not only are a child's angry outbursts viewed as intolerable in themselves, but their negativity is compounded by the angry feelings they stir up inside of us. When our kids yell out, many of us instinctively jump to silence that demon called anger. This is a mistake.

These experiences with the emotion of anger will help your child learn what it is and how it can be handled. But while he is learning, you will no doubt go through quite a few temper tantrums. Your role during a tantrum is to be calm and supportive (no easy task). Your child is feeling out of control and this can be frightening for him. He needs you to be loving but firm, and he needs to know you are still in charge and will take care of him. Never respond to a tantrum with a tantrum of your own.

Without scolding, striking, yelling, or ridiculing, pick your screamer up and try to soothe her. If that doesn't work, put her where she can't hurt herself (a time-out station is good) and wait for her to finish.

Verbalize the feeling for him. Say, "I know you're feeling angry." This will teach your child the name of his feeling and will eventually give him some control over what's happening. Don't say, "Don't be angry." Your child has every right to his feelings; he needs to learn that it's okay to be angry and talk about that anger–it's not okay to kick and scream.

Verbalize your own expectations, "You need to sit down until you feel calm." Then leave the area. Don't ever let tantrums win an argument–that gives your child a reason to continue using them. If you give in and let your child stay in the sandbox just because she made some noise, you've taught her how to use a tantrum to get her own way. Your child needs to learn that ranting and raving aren't productive ways to get what she wants.

When the tantrum is over–it's over. Don't let your own angry feelings drag on through the day. Your toddler needs to know that after a tantrum, you still love him. He needs to restore his sense of being loved. This won't encourage more tantrums in the future; it will give your child a more secure emotional base that will help him avoid tantrums down the line.

JUST A PHASE?

Keep track of the things that send your child into a fit of anger. If a child will as readily stage an angry tantrum when given a red lollipop instead of a green lollipop, as when he or she faces a real problem, the child may be using tantrums to manipulate the parents. In this case the parents need to immediately take action to reestablish their authority. (See the "Self-Control and Discipline" section under "Character Formation" later in Stage 2.)

During tranquil moments, teach your child how to prevent angry confrontations with others. Teach your child to verbalize his or her feelings. Help your child to negotiate rather than take. Show your child how to take turns and trade. (See the "Building Friendships" section under "Family and Peer Relationships" later in Stage 2.) It takes time for children to learn how to manage their anger without a temper outburst, but with your calm support, it will happen.

Parenting to Help Children Handle Joy and Anger

- Enjoy your child's outbursts of spontaneous joy.
- Expect this to be the age of the "terrible twos" and tantrums.
- Remember that tantrums are the result of frustration, not willful disobedience.
- When your child gets angry with you, let her know that you are still in charge and will take care of her.
- Give emotions verbal labels. Say, "I know you're feeling angry."

Avoid

- Thinking that toddlers throw tantrums simply to get their own way.
- Responding to a tantrum with a tantrum of your own.
- Getting into a physical battle over a tantrum. If calm words won't calm down your child, put him where he can't hurt himself (a time-out station is good) and wait for him to finish.
- Withholding your love from your child when the tantrum is over.
- Letting tantrums win an argument.

REMEMBER

Because children 18 to 36 months of age can't fully verbalize the intense emotions they feel, they need a way to vent the frustration that comes with the ongoing struggle between dependence and independence. Angry temper tantrums are the answer.

Managing Fear

In infancy, your baby experienced the emotion of fear when a stranger tried to take her from your arms and again when you left her behind with a babysitter. While children 18 to 36 months of age may still experience stranger and separation anxiety (in fact, separation anxiety will peak during this stage), the emotion of fear now takes on a broader scope as your toddler's more advanced thought processes and keener memory skills leave her open to a variety of fears.

Between the ages of 18 and 36 months it is common for children to experience developmental fears of many things that they perceive as dangerous. The list includes people who look different (e.g., uniformed police officers, clowns, and doctors), loud noises (e.g., flushing toilets and vacuum cleaners), and imaginary creatures, ghosts, and monsters. Things that your child used to love, like dogs or playground swings and slides, may also suddenly cause shrieks of terror. This about-face is no cause for alarm. If you can accept the presence of fear as a natural stage of development, your toddler will probably grow out of the fear on his or her own. Fear is a normal emotional reaction to perceived danger—don't try to make it more than that.

SCIENCE TO TAKE HOME

For children, fear is an integral part of normal development. Many fears are transitory, appear in children of similar age, and generally do not interfere with everyday functioning (Morris & Kratochwill, 1983).

When your toddler is afraid, don't deny the feeling. Don't say, "Oh, you're not afraid of bugs!" What a confusing message when your child knows for a fact that she *is* afraid of bugs! Belittling feelings will intensify your child's discomfort and can make the situation even worse. Instead, try some empathy. You might say, "I know how you feel. I used to be afraid of bugs too. But now I know they won't hurt me, so they don't bother me anymore." Your child needs to be reassured that you understand the feeling of fear and don't love her less (or think she is a "baby") for being afraid. She needs you to show respect for her feelings and at the same time offer assurances that she will learn to overcome her fear at her own pace. You might say, "It's okay if you feel scared. Why don't you just watch the bug from a distance for a while and you can move closer when you're ready." The most important lesson your child can learn from this fear is that you are there to protect the child when he or she is frightened.

JUST A PHASE?

If your child's fear keeps him or her from participating in normal daily routines like going to preschool or exploring the neighborhood, and this interrupts normal daily functioning and has continued for a week or more, your child might need professional consultation.

On the other hand, don't overreact in a well-intentioned plan to protect your child. If he screams at the sight of a bug, for example, don't sweep him up in your arms saying, "I won't let the bug hurt you. You're safe with me." Such a dramatic response tells him that there really is something to be afraid of. Instead, calmly acknowledge the fear and encourage your child to watch the bug from a safe distance as you explain that it cannot hurt her.

CONSIDER

Don't expect all children of the same age to have the same fears. Children who are shy and sensitive are likely to be more worried about dangers and more anxious of new situations than others. Just because your older child was never afraid of the dark, don't downplay the problem with your second child. It's important to respect that inborn temperament has a lot to do with how children perceive danger.

Sometimes a child's fear can be caused by abrupt family changes such as divorce, illness, or a drastic change in routine. Consider this possibility if your toddler suddenly seems fearful and can't verbalize why. Has something happened that is making him cling to you? What's on his mind that is keeping him from sleeping at night? When your child is going through a difficult time, provide extra opportunities for cuddling and talking. Use pretend play to talk about emotions and security. Patience and understanding will help your child through a transitional time that is causing him or her to be afraid.

Parenting to Help Children Handle Fear

- Remember that between the ages of 18 and 36 months it is common for children to be afraid of many things that they perceive as dangerous.
- Stay calm. Your toddler will probably grow out of the fear on his own.

AGE DIFFERENCES

Here are some of the fears that are often found in children at various age levels:

0 to 6 months	**Fear of loss of support; fear of loud noises**
7 to 12 months	**Fear of strangers; fear of sudden, unexpected, and looming objects**
1 year	**Fear of separation from parent; fear of toilets, of being injured, and of strangers**
2 years	**A multitude of fears, including fear of loud noises, animals, dark rooms, separation from parent, large objects or machines, and changes in personal environment**

- Be empathic. You might say, "I know how you feel. I used to be afraid of the dark too."
- Show respect for your child's feelings and at the same time offer assurances that she will learn to overcome her fear at her own pace.
- Encourage your child to face the object of his fear from a safe distance.
- Remember that inborn temperament has a lot to do with how children perceive danger.

REMEMBER

If you can accept the presence of fear as a natural stage of development, your toddler will probably grow out of the fear on his or her own.

Avoid

- Denying the emotion of fear by saying, "Oh, you're not afraid."
- Overreacting in a well-intentioned plan to protect your child.
- Expecting all children of the same age to have the same fears.

Cognitive Development

Scientists have found that brain development is more rapid from birth to 3 years than during any other period of life. That's what makes this such a fascinating time for toddlers, as they begin to discover that they have a mind that senses, perceives, feels, thinks, and remembers. This awareness enables them to develop problem-solving skills that help them figure out their world and their place in it. It fuels their imagination and adds a developmental component to their play. This is also a time when language emerges as a true form of self-expression and communication.

Problem Solving

Two-year-old Jannette had a problem. She wanted to play with her stuffed dog, but the dog's collar was stuck on the hinge of her toy box. First she pulled, then she pushed. Then she pulled and jumped up and down at the same time. Then she took her doll and began to hit the stuffed dog with it. When that didn't work, she began to scream. Jannette's mom rushed into the room and seeing the problem quickly solved it by freeing the collar and handing Jannette her dog–problem solved.

What Jannette's mom didn't see was the problem-solving process that Jannette herself had used to try to remedy the situation before she screamed in frustration. All her efforts to free the stuffed dog were a sign that Jannette was learning how to be a competent problem solver. Because this is the age when toddlers are just beginning to see how things work and to use memory to learn from past experiences, Jannette's mom could have used this situation to help her daughter further develop her problem-solving skills. Rather than simply free the dog herself, she might have helped Jannette to see what the problem was and then encouraged her to free the collar from the hinge.

SCIENCE TO TAKE HOME

Recall is a thinking skill that involves the remembrance of what has been learned or experienced. It is vital to the problem-solving process. The noted child developmentalist Jean Piaget argued that children do not show true recall before 1½ to 2 years of age (Piaget, 1968).

Children face problems all day long that give them lots of opportunities to practice problem-solving skills–if you let them. Look to encourage the following three kinds of problem-solving skills:

- *Means–end thinking.* This is the kind of problem solving that requires a person to figure out what steps to take to achieve a goal. A 28-month-old child, for example, might decide to pull over a chair to stand on in order to reach the cookie jar. (This may seem more dangerous than praiseworthy, but the thinking skills involved are a good sign of healthy development.)
- *Consequential thinking.* This kind of thinking skill enables a child to consider what will happen next: "If I step on a balloon, it will pop," or "If I put the smaller blocks on top of the bigger blocks I can build a tower." The realization that one thing can cause another is the thinking skill that fuels the eternal toddler question, "Why?"
- *Divergent thinking.* This is a very valuable problem-solving skill that allows a child to think of many different ways to reach the same end. "How many different ways can I use to get my sister to share her toy?"

Just as children need to exercise their muscles to make them stronger, they need to practice their thinking skills, too. When your toddler faces a problem, don't jump in to solve it too quickly. Lead your child to think about a solution. Ask questions that encourage these three kinds of thinking:

Means–End Thinking

"What do you think you could do to get your dog out of the toy box?"

"If you want to eat a banana, what should you do first?"

"To take a bath, first we'll turn on the tub water, then we'll take off your clothes. Then what should we do next?"

Consequential Thinking

"If you lift the dog's collar off this hinge, what do you think will happen?"

"If you throw your toy on the floor, what might happen to it?"

"If you give me a big hug, how will that make me feel?"

Divergent Thinking

"Pulling on your dog is one way to try to get him free. Can you think of another way?"

"Can you think of another way to make me smile?"

"What other shapes can you make with your clay?"

These three emerging problem-solving skills turn children 18 to 36 months of age into little scientists who spend their days experimenting with life. This is what problem solving is all about. It does not involve memorizing the alphabet or the names of colors and shapes. Rather, it is a skill that enables children to think both logically and creatively about their world and about the way things work. So put away the workbooks and focus instead on developmental skills that encourage the growth of means–end, consequential, and divergent problem-solving skills.

Parenting to Build Problem-Solving Skills

- Use day-to-day situations to help your child develop problem-solving skills.
- When you solve your child's problem, explain how you do it and why.
- Give your child toys like stacking and sorting toys that encourage problem solving.

AGE DIFFERENCES

Toddlers' problem-solving skills grow as their cognitive abilities mature. By about 2 years or so, the finer points of object permanence have been mastered, and in the last 6 months of their second year they can no longer be confused by difficult hiding places. By the end of the second year, children have developed representational thought—they can now think without acting. Children at this point are no longer sensorimotor in the truest sense of the term (relying solely on the information they have obtained through the senses and motor activity). They can now construct a mental image of the world, and they can defer imitation—they can see an event at one time and imitate it later (Kaplan, 1991).

- Encourage means–end thinking that helps your child figure out what steps she needs to take to achieve a goal.
- Encourage consequential thinking that enables your child to consider what will happen next.
- Encourage divergent thinking that allows your child to think of many different ways to reach the same end.

Avoid

- Solving all your child's problems before giving him a chance to think how to do it himself.
- Expecting your toddler to know how to solve daily problems without your help.
- Ridiculing your child's solution if it seems illogical to you.
- Using workbooks or skill sheets to teach problem solving. Use life situations.

REMEMBER

Just as children need to exercise their muscles to make them stronger, they need to practice their thinking skills, too. When your toddler faces a problem, lead him or her to think about a solution using means-end thinking, consequential thinking, and divergent thinking.

Play and Imagination

Your toddler's daily work is called *play*–he will spend 5 to 6 hours every day engaged in this activity. Play is an integral part of his developing physical, sensory, cognitive, and emotional makeup. As large motor skills mature he is better able to run, climb, jump, and take in new aspects of the world with all his senses. And as his reasoning skills increase, he finds joy in toys that challenge him to think. At the same time, he finds comfort and security in the world of make-believe.

The best toys for this age group are ones that capitalize on these developmental needs. For example, play materials that develop large muscle skills are most appropriate at this age. For outdoor play these children benefit from having toy ladders to climb, wagons to pull, and toy lawn mowers to push. Toys that a child can ride on are also favorites and help to develop strength and large muscle coordination.

CONSIDER

When you give your toddler clay or paint, don't expect to end up with a piece of art. These children are much more interested in the feel of the material and will spend more time squishing it between their fingers than creating a final product.

For sensory exploration, clay and its many variations provide wonderful opportunities for squeezing, squishing, and molding. Finger paints and water play (such as pouring water from one container to another and sailing boats in the bathtub) are certain to bring squeals of delight.

A child's cognitive skills are also challenged during play. Playing with things that can be put together and taken apart is great fun. Blocks are also a favorite, especially the ones that come in a variety of shapes and sizes. Sorting games, like boxes that fit inside each other or different-sized rings that stack on top of each other, all help your child think about how one thing relates to another.

You may find your toddler now clinging to a favorite doll or stuffed animal. These toys often give children a sense of emotional security, especially when they cannot be with you. If your child becomes attached to a particular "friend," don't try to talk him out of carrying it around or attempt to ditch it when he's not looking (a strong temptation when it becomes worn and tattered). He will give it up himself when it no longer serves an emotional need.

A toddler's imagination is in full swing–and what a wonderful thing it is to watch this pretend world in action. At this age, toddlers love to do household chores like you; they practice eating and drinking (before the age of 2, they may even try to eat the toy food); they play mommy and daddy with their dolls and stuffed animals. In all manner of activities, they like to imitate you.

You can encourage this kind of imaginative play by providing your children with simple pretend items like kitchen utensils, tools, garden equipment, and basic dolls. You should also give your children real-world experiences to feed their growing imaginations. A dump truck or plastic farm animal can't spark imaginative play if your child has never seen a construction site or a farm.

Pretend play is also a great way for a toddler to explore her emotions without fear of displeasing you. She can freely express anger, for

---

SCIENCE TO TAKE HOME

Although the right toys add to your child's fun and development, filling a room with age-appropriate toys is only the first step. Research studies have found that toddler play is facilitated and encouraged when a parent or teacher participates in the play. The play that results is more extended and sophisticated than would be found in children with limited access to adult play partners (Stevenson, Leavitt, Thompson, & Roach, 1988).

---

example, by hitting a doll rather than a playmate. She can transfer her own fear of the dark to a teddy bear, making it cry instead of crying herself. Your child may also experiment with feelings of tenderness by rocking and feeding a favorite stuffed animal. Or she may deal with her budding sense of right and wrong by scolding an imaginary friend. You may even see signs of empathy as she soothes her toy dog's boo-boo.

Pretend play can also help toddlers develop their cognitive skills. When your child uses a spoon to represent a telephone, for instance, he is demonstrating his ability to create symbols. Knowing how symbols work is a key factor in learning letters and numbers later on. Pretend play also helps children think logically and devise solutions (key to problem solving). Your child might, for example, build a roadway for his cars and need to move other toys out of the way in order to complete the task.

The world of make-believe is a wonderful place for your child to spend time. In the long run, researchers have found that pretend play can enhance a child's self-awareness, self-confidence, and self-control. It has also been found to have a positive influence on children's memory, language skills, and role-taking abilities (Hughes, Noppe, & Noppe, 1996).

However, in order for your child to make the most of her growing imagination, she needs time and space to pretend without interference. In other words, stay back. If she uses a paper cup as a pretend teacup, for example, you don't need to rush to the rescue with an authentic-looking tea party set. If she pushes a box around pretending it's a car, don't take it away and direct her to the toy cars in the corner. If she asks you to play school, don't automatically assume the role of teacher. This world of make-believe belongs to your child. Let her direct the show.

AGE DIFFERENCES

As toddlers' imaginations mature, you'll see a gradual change in the way children incorporate inanimate objects into their pretend play. Now they initiate make-believe actions directed, not at themselves, but at other objects. For example, instead of pretending to wash his own face as he often did when he was younger, a child might now pretend he is washing the face of his teddy bear. Toward the end of the second year of life, dolls or other inanimate objects become the initiators as well as the recipients of make-believe actions. For example, a 2-year-old child may arrange her stuffed animals around a table, put empty plates and spoons in front of them, and allow them to enjoy their meal.

This is a time when many parents excite the imaginations of their children with stories of the Easter Bunny, Santa Claus, and the like. Yet there is often a bit of concern about perpetuating such myths, which contradict a family's commitment to honesty. Don't worry. These magic myths are important symbols to children and they play a valuable role in the early years. They excite children's imagination in a positive way and allow them flights of fancy that are enriching and comforting. For example, we believe that Santa Claus symbolizes the goodwill of the whole world, a world that is in accord with your child's wishful and magical thinking. The ritualistic fantasies of childhood comfort children with the feeling that there's something or someone special just for them.

One last word about a toddler's imagination: Don't worry if your toddler creates an imaginary friend. Recent research shows that as many as 65 percent of preschoolers have imaginary friends, and the creation of such friends is associated with positive characteristics. For example, in comparison with children who don't have imaginary companions, those who do are more sociable, are less shy, have more real friends, are more creative, and participate in more family activities. Imaginary companions also seem to help children learn social skills and practice conversations. They are powerful predictors that children will play happily in nursery school and will be cooperative and friendly with peers and adults (Craig, 1996).

SCIENCE TO TAKE HOME

Does the gender of your child affect the way you encourage or discourage your child's play choices? According to research, it probably does. Beverly Fagot (1978) observed parent-child interactions in 24 families with 2-year-olds. She found that boys were allowed to play alone more often, and parents were more likely to play with boys than with girls. Girls received more praise and more criticism than boys. Both parents were more likely to stop the play activities of boys. Parents gave more positive feedback to boys when they played with blocks and more negative reaction when they played with dolls. Parents reacted more negatively when girls manipulated objects than when this was done by boys. Girls also received more positive responses when they played with dolls than did boys. Consistent with other research, fathers seemed more concerned with gender-appropriate behavior, giving more negative feedback to boys playing with dolls and other soft toys. Parents criticized girls more often when they attempted to participate in large motor activities such as running, jumping, and climbing.

Parenting to Encourage Play and Imagination

- Give your child toys that capitalize on physical, cognitive, and emotional developmental needs.
- Spend time playing with your toddler to increase the benefits derived from play.
- Encourage imaginative play by providing your children with simple pretend items like kitchen utensils, tools, garden equipment, and basic dolls.
- Give your children real-world experiences to feed their growing imaginations.
- Enjoy your child's imaginary friends. They won't be around for long.

Avoid

- Expecting your child to create works of art. The feel of the paint, clay, and even crayons is the real attraction at art time right now.
- Discouraging your child from using dolls or toys to express strong emotions. Play offers a safe way to vent strong feelings.
- Interfering with your child's world of make-believe. Even when you know how to play house better than your child does, let him or her work it out.
- Worrying about "lying" about mythical characters like Santa Claus or the tooth fairy. They excite a child's imagination in a positive way.
- Using the television as a toy. Passively watching television is not considered play.

REMEMBER

Your toddler's daily work is called *play*—he or she will spend 5 to 6 hours every day engaged in this activity. Play is an integral part of your child's developing physical, sensory, cognitive, and emotional makeup.

Language Development

Language blossoms between 18 and 36 months because these children can now think abstractly and therefore can use words as symbols for people and things. They also are now able to store these symbols in long-term memory for use at a later time. Once these two developmental milestones occur, language growth explodes.

Shortly after children turn 18 months, two-word "sentences" begin to appear in their speech. With simple statements like "More cookie," toddlers can now begin to express an amazing number of ideas.

JUST A PHASE?

The stages of language development are no more than estimations and guidelines. Many children develop their language skills at different ages and stages. Some speak volumes at an early age, while others seem indifferent to language and spend their energies learning other skills, like jumping and climbing. Some are remarkably silent until, late in toddlerhood, they suddenly begin producing full-blown language (like Albert Einstein, who didn't speak a word until he was 4 years old).

However, there are some warning signs that indicate the need for speech and hearing testing. You should seek an evaluation if any of the following applies:

- **At 18 months: no single words**
- **At 24 months: vocabulary of 10 words or less**
- **At 30 months: vocabulary of fewer than 100 words or no two-word phrases.**
- **At 36 months: vocabulary of fewer than 200 words; no sentences; clarity less than 50 percent**

To find a specialist, ask your pediatrician to recommend a speech-language pathologist or call the American Speech–Language–Hearing Association in Rockville, Maryland, for a referral (800 638 8255).

Shortly after the beginning of two-word utterances, children enter a period in which new words are learned rapidly. In fact, children learn to comprehend more than 14,000 new words, or about 9 per day, from 18 months through the preschool years (Kaplan, 1991).

After a child's second birthday, sentences usually become longer than two words, pronouns are added (especially the pronoun *I*), and plurals and past tenses of verbs are added. You'll hear the sophistication level of your child's speech change during this time:

"See truck" becomes "I see truck."

"I walk" becomes "I walked."

"See dog" becomes "I see dogs."

Toddlers' speech also reflects their growing independence. Most children quickly learn to say "No," "Mine," and "Me do it," and they practice these "sentences" often throughout each day. (Interestingly, toddlers use the word *no* many months before they can use the word *yes*.)

AGE DIFFERENCES

By 18 months, a child is using up to 20 words. By 2 years of age, the child is using up to 270 words; 2- to 3-word sentences are spoken, and the first pronouns appear. Some simple adjectives and adverbs are also present. By 30 months, the child is using up to 425 words; the child uses more adjectives and adverbs and often demands repetition from others. A child this age begins to announce intentions and ask questions. By 36 months, a child is using up to 900 words and his or her sentences are averaging 3 to 4 words per sentence. Words such as *when* and *today* show an awareness of time. The child can tell stories that can be understood. Some auxiliary forms appear, such as *can, do, did,* and *be.* The child also begins to use the word *because* (Kaplan, 1991).

Although language skills make a major leap in this short period of time, there is still a lot to learn. Before the age of 3, children have trouble with correct pronoun use. Statements like "Us going" will persist throughout this stage. These children also speak (and understand) only the active voice. Toddlers easily understand "The boy loves his dog," but they cannot grasp the concept of "The dog is loved by the boy." As they experiment with tenses and plurality, you'll still hear your children say "I comed home," or "I seed the mouses." Mispronunciations are also a consistent part of toddler speech. Children will say "boon" instead of "spoon" because they are not yet perceptually attuned to sound differences and they do not have the lip and tongue coordination to articulate better. Toddlers also use what's often called *telegraphic speech,* in which (as in telegraph messages) they leave out unimportant words such as articles, prepositions, conjunctions, and so forth; the request "Daddy, will you push me on my scooter?" becomes "Daddy, push." But all these "mistakes" are still developmental gains showing an awareness of the syntax and structure of our language.

Parenting to Encourage Language Development

- Fill in the blanks. If your child says "Truck coming," you might reply, "Yes, a big truck is coming."
- Add more information: "That's a big delivery truck."
- Use prompting to encourage vocabulary growth. Say, "Here comes a big ____." Ask your child to fill in the blank.

SCIENCE TO TAKE HOME

Studies have shown that language learning occurs when parents read to their young children. But sticking to the story line does not always get the best results. In a study by Grover Whitehurst and colleagues (1988), parents of toddlers were divided into two groups. Parents in the experimental group were instructed to (1) use open-ended questions that required the children to give more than a yes/no response, (2) encourage the children to tell more, (3) ask the children function/attribute questions (What is the farmer doing?), and (4) offer expansions (repeating statements with some additions—if a child said "Dog," the parent might say "Big dog"). Parents were also told to respond positively to the children's attempts to answer the questions and to reduce the number of questions that the children could answer by pointing. These techniques required the children to talk about the pictured materials. The control-group parents were instructed to read in their normal manner. After 1 month, children in the experimental group scored significantly higher on measures of expressive language ability and showed a higher mean length of utterance, a greater use of phrases, and a lower frequency of single words. Nine months later, the differences were somewhat less but still present.

- Read! Children learn about language by hearing it.
- Have conversations. When you talk to your child, leave a pause, giving your child a chance to respond.
- Ask your child questions (like "What?" "Where?" "When?") that require more than a yes/no response.
- Label things in the environment. When you visit a park, talk about what you see: "Look at the see-saw. I see a white swan."
- Play language games. These include playing telephone, naming pictures in a magazine, and enjoying nursery rhymes and songs.
- Simplify your speech pattern. While your child is learning the basics, use simple sentences and speak a bit more slowly than you normally do.

Avoid

- Correcting grammar mistakes; simply repeat the thought correctly. If your child says, "Truck comed," you can say, "Yes, the truck came."

- Letting your child use pointing alone as a means of communicating. When your child points to the cookie jar, for example, say "Do you want a cookie?" or "Can you say 'cookie'?"
- Being upset if your child's speech abilities regress. Language development often moves two steps forward and one step back.

REMEMBER

Children learn to comprehend more than 14,000 new words, or about 9 per day, from 18 months through the preschool years.

- Comparing your child's language development to that of other children. Verbal communication skills develop at a unique pace.
- Interpreting your child's incessant "No" response as a sign of total negativity. Very often it's just a fun word to say.
- Reading a picture book nonstop from beginning to end. Leave time to pause and talk about the story.

STAGE 2

18 to 36 Months

Family and Peer Relationships

Toddlers take their place in the family and in society with great gusto and enthusiasm—but they still are short on social graces. They love to be with children their own age, but are not yet ready to share or cooperate very often. They like to be a part of everything going on in their family, but they like things done their way—on schedule and following a secure routine. They also now begin to jostle for a place among their peers, and you'll now notice if your child seems aggressive or shy.

Building Friendships

Friendships are very important to the social and cognitive development of your child—but they can't be rushed. Children 18 to 36 months of age are still in the egocentric stage in which they believe the world revolves around them. Remember that toddlers have not yet formed a clear boundary between themselves and the outside world, and they see all property as an extension of themselves. That's why they see nothing wrong with grabbing everything in sight before their "friend" has a chance to take it away. To these toddlers, the word *sharing* means "It's mine." Because the concepts of give-and-take and mutual trust, which are the core of friendship, are just too complicated for children this age to grasp, true friendships are very rare. But this is the age in which the foundation for friendships, peer relationships, and cooperative play is established—with your help.

Keep in mind how toddlers interact with each other. Two-year-old Janet and her new friend Audrey sat happily in the sandbox digging holes, valleys, and mountains for nearly half an hour. "I thought Janet would like to play with someone her own age," says her mom, Maryann. "So I arranged this play date in the park with my friend's daughter. But the two of them haven't even looked at each other since we got here." Maryann was disappointed and assumed there was no reason to arrange another play date for these girls—but she was wrong.

Although it may not look like it, Janet and Audrey are actually enjoying each other's company. Their parallel play is typical of children in this stage. They sit side by side and pursue separate activities, sharing little verbal communication and almost no direct physical interaction. But this time together actually helps them build their social skills as they slowly take advantage of the opportunity to learn peaceful coexistence. For this reason, it's important to arrange play opportunities for your child.

When you arrange a play date, plan to make everyone comfortable. Many children this age still want their parents to stay with them—that's perfectly natural. If it raises the comfort level of the get-together, encourage the visiting mom or dad to stay. Also, limit the number of playmates: One or two toddler friends is plenty.

Because toddlers are more interested in each other's toys than in each other, when you arrange play dates, plan ahead to limit fights:

- Allow your child to put away treasured toys that cannot be shared.
- Provide duplicates of playthings such as dolls and trucks.
- Plan games and activities that can be played side by side, and prepare to offer each child his or her own set of toys such as blocks, crayons, and finger paints in order to discourage conflict.

Even when you plan ahead, however, squabbles are bound to happen between toddlers who can't yet share, so plan for them. When you see a tug-of-war begin, don't jump right in to break things up. Watch and wait a moment. The experience of pushing and pulling until someone wins the toy is often the first stage of learning how to negotiate. If it looks like somebody is going to get hurt, introduce a diversionary tactic: Bring out a new toy or change the activity. If your child can't be distracted and won't give up the idea of fighting for his "rights," don't punish him for not playing nicely. Instead, remove him from the fun for a few minutes so he can calm down and then go back and try again.

Sometimes, especially if the battle over a toy hasn't escalated to a fevered pitch, you can introduce and encourage the concept of sharing. When your child begins to battle with another child over possession of a toy, don't jump in and insist, "You must share!" Also, don't take your child's side and say to the playmate, "You shouldn't grab toys away from another child!" Instead, first acknowledge your child's feelings, then make a suggestion: "I see you want that ball all to yourself. When

SCIENCE TO TAKE HOME

You can help your child learn how to play with other children. Bhavnagri and Parke (1991) examined the effectiveness of mothers of 24-month-old toddlers in facilitating their children's play with an unfamiliar peer. In one condition two children played without assistance from an adult, while in a second condition a mother was instructed to help the children play together. On a variety of indexes of social competence (e.g., length of play, turn taking, cooperation, and altruism), children were rated significantly higher during the sessions in which their mothers assisted in play than in the sessions in which their mothers were more passive.

you're finished, how about giving it to Ken?" Or, you might say, "Would you like to play with this toy a little longer before you give it to Ken?" This kind of dialogue introduces both children to the notion of taking turns in a way that does not shame them. This won't always mediate a peace, but if you persist in putting your toddler's feelings into words for him, you'll be surprised how often he will rise to the occasion.

In calm moments, you can teach your child how to interact with playmates by encouraging them all to take turns while playing simple games (Ross, 1982). These games might include the following:

- Stacking and tumbling three foam blocks.
- Putting wooden blocks into a pail and dumping them out.
- Hiding and finding a ball under a blanket.
- Covering one's face with a hat for the other child to uncover (peek-a-boo).
- Rolling a ball back and forth. (This illustrates the idea that what you share eventually comes back.) Give immediate praise when your child does share something.

After each play date, take some time to evaluate the good and bad. What activities should you repeat next time? Which ones should you drop? Do the children enjoy building towers with blocks or running and jumping? Plan to structure your next play date around activities that nurture fun, allow for parallel play, and introduce the idea of cooperative play.

CONSIDER

You shouldn't make toddlers share toys they think are rightfully theirs. Children have a right to a sense of ownership. If you respect children's need to have their own things and don't force the idea of sharing, you may actually get children to stop arguing faster and share more often in the long run.

Also, evaluate your own involvement: You should help your child learn how to interact with others; you certainly should stop harmful actions like biting and hitting; and you should always be in the room to supervise. But this doesn't mean that you must always be on the floor in the middle of all play. When your toddler becomes familiar with her new playmate, it's time to step back a bit so your child can learn to be comfortable–on her own–in close proximity to an age mate.

Parenting to Help Children Develop Friendships

- Remember that parallel play is typical of children this age.
- Arrange play dates for your child.
- Plan ahead to limit fights by allowing your child to put away treasured toys and by planning side-by-side activities like coloring and block building.
- To keep the peace, use diversionary tactics or remove your child from the fun for a few minutes until she calms down.
- Introduce and encourage the concept of sharing (but don't expect it to actually happen very often).
- Teach your child how to interact with playmates by encouraging them all to take turns while playing simple games.
- Structure play dates around activities that nurture fun, allow for parallel play, and introduce the idea of cooperative play.

Avoid

- Expecting your child to frequently engage in cooperative, interactive play.
- Inviting too many toddlers to a play date. Let your child get used to one friend before adding another.
- Breaking up a squabble immediately; let the children try to figure it out themselves at first.
- Insisting, "You must share!" Instead, first acknowledge your child's feelings, then make a suggestion.
- Making a toddler share a toy he thinks is rightfully his.

REMEMBER

This is the age in which the roots of friendships, peer relationships, and cooperative play begin to form—with your help.

- Leaving toddlers alone when they play. Always be present to supervise.
- Insisting on being right in the middle of toddlers' play. Give them room to work things out themselves.

Family Rituals and Routines

No two hectic mornings are alike at the Haycock home. Sometimes Jane drops off 2½-year-old Arleen at her grandmother's house on the way to work. Sometimes, Arleen's dad hurriedly packs her up and brings her to the day-care facility by his office. And sometimes, Arleen spends her day playing at a neighbor's home. But whatever the arrangement, Arleen always screams when it's time to leave the house. "She throws a fit every morning," says Jane, "when it's time to say goodbye."

Most toddlers don't like to be separated from their parents, but for children like Arleen, the lack of a consistent routine makes the separation even more difficult. Children in this stage demand order and predictability. They like everything to be in its place, and what they did yesterday, they want to do again today. For this reason, lack of routine increases the number and the frequency of temper explosions among children in this age group.

Knowing that children this age need an ordered routine to feel safe and secure, you can plan ahead to make life a bit more predictable. If the Haycocks, for example, can't make consistent childcare arrangements, they can still help their daughter feel secure in that particular routine. Children in this situation need to know the night before where they're going the next day, when they'll go, who will take them, what they'll do while they're there, and who will pick them up. Arleen's parents might make a large calendar that lets Arleen put stars on the days she'll be with Grandma, flowers on the days she'll go to day care, and happy faces on the days she'll stay at her neighbor's. This takes the surprise and trauma out of the morning rush by acknowledging the child's developmental need for order.

This same need for predictability carries over to the daily schedule. Your child will feel more secure and empowered if she follows a daily routine. Knowing when you will wake, eat, play, and go to bed may seem regimented to you, but to a toddler it's reassuring. Because toddlers can't tell time, it's not necessary to tightly schedule every activity by the clock, but it is helpful if one activity routinely follows another. The early part of the day, for example, may include outdoor playtime, followed by lunch, followed by quiet indoor play, followed by a nap. This simple routine helps a child know what's coming next—and this is very important when you're just beginning to figure out how your world works.

JUST A PHASE?

Obsessive-compulsive adults have a psychological disorder that compels them to do the same things in the same order all the time. Do not worry when your toddler prefers a particular schedule and throws a fit if his or her routine is changed. This insistence on order and sameness is a normal developmental stage.

Actually, the need for an orderly routine can become a rigid demand between 18 and 36 months. Your child may insist, for example, that his shoes go on before his coat; breaking this order is cause for a major tantrum. He may refuse to eat if someone sits in the "wrong" seat at the dinner table. He may become frightened and confused if you take a new route to the babysitter's. When these things happen, try to understand—this stage won't last forever, and it will pass with less upset if you give your child the predictability he needs.

Routines that become ritualized (i.e., have a ceremony attached) can help a toddler get through transitional situations (such as going to nursery school or going to bed) that can be scary. You might, for example, create a goodbye tradition in which you sing a few lines of a favorite song, then give a hand squeeze, a smile, and a kiss. You might even offer a swatch of your old pajamas scented with your favorite perfume or cologne to bind the ritual to you. Before bedtime, you might habitually give a goodnight kiss, sing a song, read a book, and turn on the night-light. A ritual's repetitive predictability helps toddlers feel secure and steady.

When you create a ritualistic routine, make sure it's one that you're willing to repeat and can pass on to the child's caregivers. If you don't want to kiss all your child's stuffed animals, and sing six songs, and read five stories every night—don't do it. Once a ritual is established, it's very difficult to break. Also, make sure to tell your child's caretakers about the rituals you use. If you go out and forget to tell the babysitter about the bedtime ritual, he or she will be in for a long night of crying. If your child's grandparent is going to take the child to nursery school and he or she doesn't know about the goodbye ritual, there may be separation tears at the door.

Parenting to Create Rituals and Routines

- Plan ahead to make life more predictable for your toddler.
- Try to understand your toddler's need to do things the same way every time.
- Use ritualized routines to help your child get through transitional moments, such as going to the babysitter or going to sleep.
- Give your child a sense of control and security by organizing the child's day according to a predictable routine.

Avoid

- Scheduling so tightly that you become a slave to the clock. Consistency of activities is what's important.
- Worrying that a toddler's insistence on a brief ritual is a sign of an obsessive-compulsive disorder.
- Creating a ritual that you don't want to always repeat or that you can't pass on to other caregivers.

REMEMBER

Children 18 to 36 months of age demand order and predictability. They like everything to be in its place, and what they did yesterday, they want to do again today.

Peer Pressure

To help sort out positive from negative peer pressure, kids need the balancing influence of their parents. They need to know what their moms and dads believe. They need to know that some values can't be sacrificed to the crowd, and they need to know they have a solid base of support and understanding back home. These lessons start early, between 18 and 36 months of age.

Two-and-a-half-year-old Leonard was playing happily with his new truck when his three-year-old cousin, Aaron, grabbed it away from

CONSIDER

Although toddlers engage primarily in parallel play with their friends, they still are open to the influence of peer pressure. If they often play with a child who is rough and loud, their own play may soon mimic this style. If they play with someone who hits and bites, they too may do the same. This is peer pressure to conform at its earliest stage.

him. "I didn't know what to do," confessed Leonard's mom. "On the one hand I think he has a right to play with his new toy, but on the other, I want him to share with his cousin." Should Leonard's mom give the truck back to him, or tell Leonard he has to let Aaron have a turn?

Every parent faces this dilemma when kids start to play together. But who finally gets the truck isn't really the big question–it's how that decision is made that matters. As children gradually learn the rhythms of give-and-take from each other, watch how they respond to peer pressure. Does your child give in easily to please others? Does your child bully other children to get his way? Does your child stand up for herself? These behaviors are all tactics children employ to handle their peers. Now is a good time to teach your child some basic skills that help even little ones deal with peer pressure.

AGE DIFFERENCES

At times, young toddlers play completely oblivious to what's happening around them and are not influenced by their playmates. But as they approach their second birthday, peer pressure becomes more notable and influential. In fact, you can use it at this time in a positive way. Many children will use the potty, for example, because they want to be "big," like older siblings or friends.

Budding language skills help in this process. You can teach toddlers how to negotiate with their peers for what they want. Aaron can be told to ask for the truck. Leonard can be taught to say that he's not finished playing with it yet. If Aaron grabs it anyway, Leonard can be coached to stand up for himself and ask for it back. If Leonard refuses to ever share the truck, it's time to teach Aaron how to negotiate. He might be encouraged to offer a trade, or to suggest a time limit. As soon as a toddler is able to talk, be sure that you teach him to "use his words" to say "No" or "It's mine" to share how he's feeling, instead of hitting or biting.

To evaluate the peer pressure your child might be experiencing, observe how your child and her playmates interact. Is your child constantly being pressured to give in? If so, peer pressure is already having a negative effect. In this case, it's time to find a new playmate whose age, temperament, and social skills are a better match for your child's. If it's your child who is doing the pressuring, you should start teaching her empathy. Try asking, "How would you feel if Sara hit you?" These kind of early lessons in empathy can keep young children from growing into the neighborhood bully.

As your children learn how to talk, teach them to speak up for themselves. Tell them what to say and then let them try it. This will set the groundwork for skills they'll use to handle negative peer pressure as they get older.

Don't dismiss peer pressure as totally negative. Positive peer pressure plays a significant role in influencing a toddler's behavior. A child in nursery school who is not toilet trained will likely try to imitate his peers who do not have to wear diapers. He will also learn how to do things like building a castle out of blocks by watching others, and he'll learn the value of sharing by the way his peers treat him when he does or does not. Peer influence also encourages the growth of language development. Peer pressure can actually help you guide your child in the right direction.

Parenting to Help Children Deal with Peer Pressure

- Expect your toddler to mimic the play style of playmates.
- Watch how your child responds to peer pressure–passively or actively.
- Teach toddlers how to negotiate with their peers for what they want.
- Find playmates whose age, temperament, and social skills are a good match for your child's.

REMEMBER

Although toddlers engage primarily in parallel play with their friends, they still are open to the influence of peer pressure. Children between 18 and 36 months of age can be taught to use language to respond to this pressure.

Avoid

- Completely condemning peer pressure–sometimes it can be positive.
- Letting more aggressive playmates push your child around.
- Letting your child push other children around. Instead, offer lessons in empathy.

Personal Growth

Between the ages of 18 and 36 months, toddlers take gigantic leaps in personal growth. They begin to define themselves both internally and externally and to learn how they fit in the world as separate and unique human beings. Instead of running away when they are angry, for example, they will now dig in their heels, refuse to budge, and yell "No!" These children are ready to assert that they want to be in control of what they do and don't do. They now have a sense of self, a need for autonomy, and the ability to take on some responsibility.

Sense of Self

As children begin to recognize themselves as people separate from everyone else, the parents' goal is to help them establish a sense of self as lovable and competent individuals. Knowing the signs of emerging individuality will help you nurture your child's sense of self, rather than squash it.

CONSIDER

Toddlers take negative and positive assessments of themselves very seriously, so be careful what you say. Parental comments about their abilities and appearance will affect the way young children view themselves.

Who Am I?

By 18 months you will see signs of blossoming self-identification when your toddler is able to state her name and point out her own picture from a group of toddlers. By the end of the second year, you will see further evidence of your child's growing sense of self:

- His language will become filled with references to self. The words *me* and *mine* assume new importance.
- She will often describe her needs and feelings in the third person by saying something like, "Katie wants water."
- The concept of ownership is clearly and strongly acted out. (Perhaps sharing is not on toddlers' lists of things to do because they need to establish a concept of ownership in order to clarify their definition of self.)

SCIENCE TO TAKE HOME

In one study of 2-year-olds playing in pairs, most of them began their play with numerous self-assertions. They defined their boundaries and their possessions—"My shoe, my doll, my car." The author of this study asserts that this is a cognitive achievement, not necessarily selfishness: The children are increasing their self-understanding and their understanding of the other child as a separate being. A review of other studies of children's self-concepts and social play concluded that children who are most social also have a better developed self-concept. Thus, self-understanding is closely linked to the child's understanding of the social world (Craig, 1996).

- He becomes fearful of injury and may want to wear many Band-Aids.
- She shows signs of hurt feelings. A toddler may pucker her facial muscles and seem close to tears if insulted by being brushed aside, for example.
- He shows signs of self-consciousness. A child may look around to see if he is noticed, call attention to himself, or avert his eyes or head as though embarrassed.
- She becomes self-assertive. Every time a toddler says no, she is testing her powers of assertion in opposition to another person.

Gender Identity

After toddlers attain a sense of self (somewhere between 18 and 24 months) they add another dimension to their identity: gender. By 2½, children can label themselves and other people as boys or girls, but they are still confused about the meaning of being male or female. They believe gender can change by changing clothes, for example, and they may think it is possible that their sex will change someday. But don't let this tenuous grasp of gender identity worry you. It's perfectly all right for boys to play with dolls and girls to play with trucks. There's no need to steer your child to same-sex friends; they will happily play with either sex right now. There's no cause for alarm if your son wants to dress up like Mommy; it's natural for a toddler to want to imitate the opposite-sex parent by dressing like him or her. Eventually, children gain a secure

CONSIDER

Don't let sexual stereotypes interfere with your children's choices of toys to play with. Their choices at this age do not reflect their sexual orientation or identity. It is helpful for young children to explore all parts of themselves—the sensitive and caring and the rough and reckless.

sense of their gender identity, but right now, they're still coming to terms with the idea.

Children solidify their understanding of the concept of male and female by watching the people around them and by imitating what they see. Sara remembers the day she was surprised by her children's concept of gender. She had brought her 2-year-old twins, Alicia and Mike, to visit a friend across town. As they opened the backyard gate, Alicia ran over to play with the toy baby carriage and Mike grabbed the toy lawn mower. "I couldn't believe my eyes!" remembers Sara. "I had always given them both the same playthings without any gender labels." But here, with the freedom to choose, Alicia chose the "girl's" toy and Mike chose the "boy's." Why?

Although Sara may have carefully chosen her children's toys to avoid gender bias, her children have reached a developmental stage where they want to imitate basic daily routines that they see often and with which they have personal experience. Apparently, in their home, these twins see their mom take care of children and their dad mow the lawn.

As in so many other areas of development, what you say will help mold a child's sense of self, but what you do will have an even greater impact.

Self-Esteem

At first, toddlers build a sense of self that is very objective: I am a person; I am separate from others; I am a boy/girl. But eventually, they build a self-image that is based on subjective evaluation of themselves: Children will decide if they are good or bad; lovable or unlovable; attractive or unattractive; smart or dumb. Many of these judgments are picked up from the people around them. You can bolster your child's self-esteem in many simple ways throughout the course of each day:

- When you discipline your child, focus on the behavior, not the child. Instead of saying "You're a bad boy," or "Good girls don't do that," say "Biting someone is bad because it hurts them."
- Seek your child's opinion often.
- Openly express affection.
- Establish and enforce guidelines for your child. (See the "Self-Control and Discipline" section under "Character Formation" later in Stage 2.)

This is the stage when a young person tries to answer the question, "Who am I?" The answer will depend on how you respond to your child's increasing need to be a person who is separate from you, who can think independently, and who, at the same time, needs unconditional love and support.

Parenting to Help Children Develop a Sense of Self

- Know the signs of emerging individuality so you can nurture rather than squash it.
- Be careful what you say about your toddler–the child will take it to heart.
- Let your children play with any toys they like, without concern for their "gender appropriateness."
- Be aware that your child learns about gender roles from your example.
- Bolster your child's self-esteem in many simple ways throughout the course of each day.

Avoid

- Confusing self-assertions with selfishness. Saying "It's mine" is a good sign of growing individuality.
- Expecting your child to be free of gender stereotypes if your lifestyle sets a contrary example.
- Labeling your child as good or bad.
- Using nicknames like "Chubby" or "Shorty" that can create body image problems.
- Comparing your child to other children. Don't say "Why can't you finish your puzzle like Tommy?"

REMEMBER

As children begin to recognize themselves as people separate from everyone else, the parents' goal is to help them establish a sense of self as lovable and competent individuals.

Autonomy

The central theme of development during toddlerhood is autonomy: becoming aware of oneself as a person among other people and wanting to do things for oneself. Although grasping for autonomy is a natural, normal, and positive developmental step, it can also be exasperating for both children and parents. As children gain a sense of autonomy, they incessantly try their parents' patience because they begin to insist on having things their own way. Often daily battles are fought over things like what foods to eat, when to go to bed, when to end playtime, or when, where, and how a toddler can explore. It's the drive for autonomy that causes the negative, stubborn behavior that is the root of many temper tantrums and power struggles.

Two-year-old Danny Hall is a good illustration of growing autonomy and the problems it can cause. Danny is into everything–closets, drawers, and cabinets are his favorite playthings. So, needless to say, Danny's dad, George, is forever on damage-control duty directly behind him. "My boy is going to think his name is 'No, Danny,' " laughs George, "because that's all I ever say to him." But if George continually walks behind his son, stopping him, redirecting him, and scolding him, it won't be long before Danny throws himself on the floor in a screaming fit that says, "Leave me alone!"

Children this age are very curious; they love to explore, and they do cause trouble. But George's constant protective interruptions are invading Danny's need to have some control over his actions and his environment. So what's a parent to do? In this instance, George might acknowledge his son's need for independent exploration by setting up safe zones in various parts of the house. A *safe zone* is an area where you've removed the locks and dangerous objects from selected drawers, closets, and cabinets (such as the pots and pans section of the kitchen cabinets), so you can then stand back. Independent exploration can get a bit messy, but it's a wonderful way to give children some room to feel in charge, while keeping an eye out for their well-being from a distance.

AGE DIFFERENCES

- **A 1-year-old will usually hold out her arms when her parents are trying to dress her.**
- **A 2-year-old may cross his arms tightly across his chest and refuse to cooperative at all in the dressing routine.**
- **A 3-year-old will often actively participate in the getting-dressed routine.**

The struggle for autonomy also shows itself in one of the toddler's favorite words: *no.* Some parents see this word as a defiant threat to their own authority and move to immediately teach their children that "backtalk" will not be tolerated. But severe discipline for saying no delivers the wrong message at this age. It teaches a child that using words to express independent wishes is unacceptable to parents. As parents, we need to understand that a toddler's negative response is a sign of normal development. Noshpitz and King (1991) explain:

> To distinguish himself as a person, the child must define a difference, indicate a boundary, draw a line. The easiest way to assert non-dependence is to be noncompliant, to do the opposite of what someone else expects. Hence, whatever the mother may ask of the child, he says: "No!" In negativism there is a declaration of selfhood, which is what the child seeks with his defiance. It is the easiest way for the child to declare his separateness and assert a modicum of independence.

Misunderstanding a child's need to achieve autonomy also is the cause of many power struggles. Children who feel they have no control over anything will fight against almost everything their parents want them to do. But you'll find that if you provide some areas where your child can be boss, you'll create a better balance of power that satisfies a child's need for some control. Choose some broad areas in which your child can make important decisions–like what to have for snacks, or what kind of toys to play with, or what kind of clothes to wear. Making decisions is tough work, so children need opportunities to practice and lots of praise for the effort. Of course, you might not like your child's choice of mismatched socks, so make it easy on both of you by limiting the choices. Let your child decide between two lunch items, or two outfits, or two toys. Then praise whichever one he chooses. As your child feels in control of some aspects of his life, you may see a surprising change in his willingness to cooperate in other areas.

SCIENCE TO TAKE HOME

Children who feel comfortable making small decisions when they're very young have an advantage when they're older and have to make larger decisions, simply because they've had more practice and broader experience to draw from (Kutner, 1994).

The drive for autonomy also introduces the "me-do-it" stage. This can make the simplest tasks infuriatingly messy and slow, but try to have patience. The battle for independence is slowly won. Often, a child's abilities fall short of her desire, so although she wants to dress herself, she can't yet manage the buttons and ties, or always distinguish the front from the back. This alone can bring on a tantrum. Yet when you offer to help, you're treated like the enemy. The challenge for parents is to find ways to help children with the tasks they're not able to do without taking over the ones they are capable of doing themselves.

To encourage autonomy and keep your sanity at the same time, try these tips the next time your toddler insists, "Me do it":

- *Take turns.* Let your child have a try at it all by herself. Then step in and ask if you can have a turn.
- *Give some room.* Even when you know your child can't complete a task, don't rush in too quickly to take over. Give him time to try and even to feel frustrated for a bit; frustration teaches persistence.
- *Make some adjustments.* Try to make the task more child-friendly. If, for example, your daughter wants to pour the milk into her own cereal bowl, give her a small cup of milk to pour from.
- *Slow down.* We're all in a hurry all the time, but toddlers can't do things as quickly as we can. So leave more time in your schedule for waiting around while your toddler does things for himself. If, for example, he insists on putting on his own shoes as you're running out the door, plan to start that task 10 minutes earlier than usual next time.

The next time you offer help and your child pushes you away, don't get insulted. Instead, feel glad that she is developmentally right on track.

Parenting to Nurture Autonomy

- Accept your child's need for independent exploration by creating safe zones in your house.
- Remember that a toddler's negativity is a sign of normal development.
- Provide your child with some areas where he or she can be boss.
- Choose broad areas in which your child can make important decisions.
- Give your child lots of opportunities to practice making decisions and praise the effort.
- Help your children with the tasks they're not able to do without taking over the ones they are capable of doing themselves.

JUST A PHASE?

Although most toddlers want to do things for themselves, there are some overdependent toddlers who need help becoming autonomous. If your toddler looks to you to solve all his problems, to complete all her tasks, to feed him his food, and even to sit down and play all her games with her, he or she may need a little prodding out of the nest. Try these two simple strategies:

- ***Work side by side.*** **If he always wants you to put on his shoes, offer to put on one while he puts on the other. If he wants you to build a castle of blocks, offer to build one while he builds another.**
- ***Start and then leave.*** **If she won't even try to begin a project without your help, start doing it, but then explain that you have to leave the room for just a moment, and encourage your child to keep working while you're gone. For example, start putting the cape back on the action hero (for the hundredth time that day), but then hand it to your child as you leave, asking her to try to finish the job. When you return, give great praise for anything that's been done in your absence.**

Avoid

- Constantly standing behind your children, stopping them, redirecting them, and scolding them.
- Getting angry when your child practices the idea of saying no.
- Creating a situation in which your child will make an unacceptable decision by asking broad questions such as "What do you want to eat?" Instead, give a choice between two acceptable foods.
- Rushing in to help your child complete a task. Give your child time to try to work it out.
- Always taking over a task because you're in a hurry and you can do it faster.
- Getting insulted when your child refuses your offer of help.
- Encouraging your child to remain dependent on you. Encourage autonomy.

REMEMBER

Although striving for autonomy is a natural, normal, and positive developmental step, it can also be exasperating for both children and parents.

Responsibility

What has your child done today to show a sense of responsibility? Has he picked up his toys? Has she fed the dog? Has he washed his own hands? Has she brought you the mail? If you can't think of any responsible task your child has accomplished today, he or she has missed out on the opportunity to feel valuable and competent. Developmentally, children between 18 and 36 months of age are no longer helpless, totally dependent, or unskilled. They are ready, willing, and able to learn about responsibility.

Lessons in responsibility can begin by teaching young children to accept the consequences of their actions. If your son spills his drink, for example, hand him the paper towel to clean it up (even if you go back later to complete the job). If your daughter scatters the puzzle pieces around the room, make sure she picks them up before she takes out another toy. Learning to take responsibility for one's actions is a valuable life lesson.

Young children can also learn to be responsible for personal cleanliness. With supervision, most 2-year-olds can wash and dry their hands. They can put their soiled clothes in the washing machine and add a cup of detergent. They can get into the tub and make some strokes across their bodies with a washcloth.

Having assigned chores helps toddlers exercise their thinking skills, memory power, and organizational systems, as well. When a young child is instructed to put a napkin by every place setting for dinner, for example, he needs to find the napkins, figure out how many he needs, and put them in the right spots. When a child is asked to water the plants (with a lightweight watering can), she must first remember to fill the watering can with water and then remember where each plant is located. Doing these kinds of simple chores is a great way to foster a child's need for autonomy while at the same time teaching responsibility.

When you introduce the idea of doing chores around the house, follow these guidelines:

- Make sure it is age-appropriate. Your 2-year-old is not yet ready to vacuum the rugs, but he is ready to dust with a cloth. Your 28-month-old isn't old enough to give the dog a bath, but she can add the soap to the water and help you suds up the dog's fur.

- Break the task down into small pieces. "Clean this room" is too broad a request. Say specifically what you want done: "Pick up the dirty clothes and put them in the hamper."
- Do the chore together at first. Later, when your child has mastered the task, let him or her try it independently.
- Keep chore time fun by singing songs or telling stories as you work.
- Give lots of praise for a job well done (or at least done).

The hardest part of teaching your child responsibility is cleaning up after he or she has lent a helping hand. You can do these tasks much faster, neater, and better than your child, and so it's very tempting to just do them yourself and get it over with. But that kind of attitude gives us a world full of kids who are self-centered and irresponsible. Children need the chance to practice helping others and doing things for themselves. Don't cheat your child out of this opportunity. Whether your child is 18 months or 3 years old, he or she should be given areas of responsibility–for dressing and caring for himself, for looking after her own possessions, for doing small tasks around the house. This is how a healthy attitude toward doing one's part is learned.

Parenting to Teach Responsibility

- Teach your child to accept the consequences of his or her actions.
- Give your child some responsibility for personal cleanliness.
- Give your child a daily chore to teach responsibility as well as to exercise thinking skills, memory power, and organizational systems.
- Show your child how the chore is to be done. Work together at first.
- Commend your child for completing tasks.

Avoid

- Always cleaning up after your child. Give her a chance to be responsible for her own messes.
- Assigning chores that are too difficult for your child.
- Assigning chores that are too general, such as "Clean this room." Break each job into small pieces.
- Rushing in to do everything for your child because it's faster and better if you do it yourself.

REMEMBER

Developmentally, children between 18 and 36 months of age are no longer helpless, totally dependent, or unskilled. They are ready, willing, and able to learn about responsibility.

Character Formation

Just as toddlers are learning that they are separate from you, that they exist as individuals, they are also developing the character traits that will define them as unique persons. Now is the time when toddlers begin to understand that some things are right and others wrong. They are learning that their actions affect the way others feel and that there are boundaries and limits that dictate what they can and can't do. They can also now learn how to be treat others with respect and how to be polite. These lessons build the character that will identify them for years to come. You'll quickly find, however, that at this age these lessons are learned very slowly, requiring much repetition and patience on your part.

Values and Morals

All societies have a system of rules about the rightness and wrongness of certain behaviors. A child is expected to learn these rules and to experience emotional discomfort or guilt when violating them and satisfaction when conforming to them. This is how personal values and morals are developed.

The process of developing values and morals begins with the creation of a conscience–that inner voice that guides our choices and decisions based on what's good and right. The roots of conscience are seeded between the ages of 18 and 36 months as a toddler's awareness of the world expands to include a knowledge that some things and actions are good and some are bad. Only now is she beginning to notice that there are negative changes in her world. Perhaps a toy is broken, a favorite item has disappeared, or her mother's face looks sad. The child registers the change and shows her displeasure by making a disapproving face or sound, or even by throwing a tantrum. The child is developing the ability to observe that the world is governed by rules and to protest when the rules are broken. This developmental leap is a forerunner of the child's ability to understand that moral standards and personal values exist.

This awareness if further supported each time your toddler gets feedback about which of her actions please you and which ones do not. Based on the information she receives, your child gets a sense of how she *should* behave—of what's right and what's wrong, what's good and what's bad. This is the foundation of personal values and morals that you can support and encourage in your toddler.

Most often toddlers are motivated to do what's right by external motivators—to reap rewards or to avoid punishment. In fact, most children do not operate out of a clear understanding of right and wrong, versus a fear of getting caught, until at least the age of 10. But that doesn't mean they can't begin to acquire an inner moral voice that helps them make decisions based on what's right and what's wrong, rather than what will earn a scolding and what will earn a smile.

SCIENCE TO TAKE HOME

Martin Hoffman (1963) and other researchers have shown that parents who consistently react to their children's misbehavior by focusing the child's attention on the feelings of the person the child has harmed tend to have children who evince a better understanding of other people's perspectives and who are more empathic and altruistic.

Your child will develop a moral voice when he learns to internalize the rules of right and wrong. You can help him do this by offering reasons for your rules. Rather than repeatedly insisting, "Don't hit your sister!" you should explain why: "You hurt your sister when you hit her and this makes her feel sad. Do not hit her." The lesson here is not to change a behavior because it makes the parent angry, but rather to change because of the way it affects others. When a child won't share, don't insist "You must be nice and give Bobby the toy now." Instead, give a moral reason: "Bobby wants to have fun, too; we share toys so everyone can be happy." These explanations help children learn to do what's right not only to avoid punishment, but because they understand the feelings of others.

The appearance of empathy is also a sign of moral development. It is empathy that allows us to feel pleasure at other people's joy and pain at their suffering. This is a prerequisite to the development of a conscience.

You'll now see occasional signs of empathy in your young child. If a friend falls off a playground swing, for example, he may cry, too. If your child sees that you are sad, she may offer you the comfort of her favorite doll. This ability to feel what another person is feeling appears to be an inborn developmental trait that occurs without prompting.

Although the ability to feel empathy is innate, it needs parental encouragement to grow strong. You can nurture the growth of empathy in your child by talking about feelings:

- Give feelings names, such as happy, sad, angry, afraid, and so on.
- Acknowledge your own feelings. If you are upset, don't always try to put on a happy face for your child. Admit, "I feel angry right now."
- Identify feelings in others. If you see a child laughing, ask your child how he or she thinks that child feels.
- Talk about the feelings that can be identified by facial expressions in storybooks or television movies.

CONSIDER

How you discipline your toddler can determine the pattern of the child's moral thinking. While loud scolding and stern disciplinary measures can frighten a child into obedience, such approaches may also contribute to a conscience that is organized around fear of consequences instead of genuine caring and regard for others.

You can also promote empathy through pretend play. Assign feelings to your child's dolls and stuffed animals. Tell your child that you think Fuzzy is unhappy and needs a hug. Don't hesitate to hug the toy, or kiss a boo-boo, or clap and laugh to share your happiness. Encourage your child to take care of her doll's feelings, hold it close when it's sad, make it jump up and down when it's happy. These kinds of games help children recognize feelings in others and respond to those feelings.

The conscience is slow to develop. Although your child may understand that another person is hurt or feels bad, that may not yet be enough to push him to show compassion. When the friend in the previous example falls off a playground swing, don't be surprised if your toddler does not offer sympathy, but rather steps on the injured child in his rush to get on the swing that's now vacant. And although your child may come to understand that hitting his sister hurts her, all bets are off if she grabs a favorite toy out of his hands. Children this age are still too egocentric to curb their impulses and put the feelings of others before their own, but they're ready to start learning how it's done.

Parenting to Teach Values and Morals

- Remember that toddlers are most often motivated to do what's right by external motivators like rewards and punishments.
- Help your child develop an inner moral voice by offering reasons for your rules.

- React to your child's misbehavior by focusing his attention on the feelings of the person he has harmed.
- Look for occasional signs of empathy in your child.
- Encourage the growth of empathy by talking about feelings.
- Promote empathy through pretend play.

REMEMBER

The roots of conscience are seeded between the ages of 18 and 36 months as a toddler's awareness of the world expands to include a knowledge that some things and actions are good and some are bad.

Avoid

- Making rules for your child to follow without giving a reason for the rule.
- Using loud scoldings and stern disciplinary measures to frighten a child into obedience.
- Expecting your toddler always (or even often) to show her compassionate side.

Self-Control and Discipline

Because this is the age of obstinance, negativism, and egocentrism, discipline is usually a subject of concern for parents of toddlers. Some institute a very strict discipline style to nip rebellion in the bud. Others worry that too many restrictions will inhibit a child's natural curiosity and so they let children do whatever they like. Unfortunately, both of these parenting styles invite trouble. Children will best learn self-control through discipline that falls somewhere in the middle ground between the two extremes of very strict and permissive. (See Stage 3 for more information on the three types of disciplinary styles.)

When you think about disciplining your child, think about the meaning of the word *discipline.* It comes from the same Latin root that means *disciple*–"one who learns." This is key to understanding that discipline is more about teaching and protecting than it is about scolding and punishment. Eventually, the self-control of a disciplined child comes from within, even when there is no adult there to scold. Therefore the goal of discipline is not to create an obedient child; instead, it is twofold: (1) to teach the child right from wrong, and (2) to enable the child to develop enough self-control to function happily and effectively in this world. Now is the right time to guide your child toward these goals. If the idea of right and wrong is not introduced until a child is 4 or 5, it will be very difficult for the child to internalize this information.

There are a variety of disciplinary tactics that can help you point your young child in the right direction. Most toddler problems can be handled with a disciplinary approach that relies on a few environmental changes. To protect your child (and your home), be sure to safety proof the areas where your child is free to explore and to move all valuables to high places. You will not stop a toddler's curiosity by saying "Don't touch" all day long. This is not discipline; it's systematic aggravation.

In circumstances where your child digs in her heels and is ready for a fight, try distraction before a confrontation. Bring out a favorite toy, draw attention to a new activity, put on some dance music. Very often she'll gladly call a truce and move on without a fight.

Give a hug and a kiss. Toddler upsets are often caused by frustration and are remedied with comfort and reassurance. A scolding just fuels the fire; a kiss makes it all better.

While using these disciplinary tactics to *avoid* trouble, you can also teach your child what she can and can't do by setting limits. *Limits* are rules that give structure to a toddler's world and help her feel secure in much the same way that routines make the world manageable. Consistent limits teach children what is expected of them and how they should behave. Although toddlers may not appear to like the idea of rules, without limits their world is too overwhelming and uncontrollable. After repeatedly testing you to see if you really mean what you say, your child will learn that she can count on certain things, like safety rules and bedtime.

The limits you set should always be clear, consistent, and fair. Whenever you make a rule, test it against these factors:

- *Be clear.* A toddler's language skills are still weak. Do not make your rules too long or too verbal. Make them clear and simple. Say "It hurts the dog when you pull her tail. Do not do that."
- *Be consistent.* If your child cannot have junk food before dinner, the rule must be enforced always. If you sometimes give in, you create a problem that will drive you crazy. It's like working a slot machine–your child quickly learns that if he keeps whining and crying, every so often the effort will pay off.
- *Be fair.* If your child continually breaks every rule you make, you may have too many rules or inappropriate rules. A toddler's memory is just now getting into gear; it's impossible for your child to

remember all the dos and don'ts of the world, so limit the number you expect her to remember to perhaps two or three that really matter. And make sure they are age-appropriate. If you set a rule that requires your toddler to sit at the table until all family members are finished eating, for example, you're asking for trouble.

Two methods you can use to enforce the family rules are praise and punishment. *Praise* is the more powerful motivator because it is a form of attention that all young children crave. The need for attention is so strong right now that toddlers will often misbehave the moment you pick up the phone because this takes your attention away from them. When you scold them for annoying you while you were on the phone, they win what they wanted all along, because even negative attention is better than none at all. When you see your child being good, stop and praise the effort. For example, say, "It's so good to see you being nice to your little sister." If you do this consistently, you'll reduce the amount of times you have to scold your child for mistreating his sister.

Punishment is another rule enforcer, but it should be used far less frequently than praise. Punishment is a consequence; it is not abuse. If your child hits another child, she should be removed from the play area; she should not be hit herself. If your child throws food on the floor, he should be scolded and removed from the table; he should not be sent to his room for the night without any more food or attention. Removing your child from the immediate area is a very effective disciplinary tactic called *time-out*. It immediately interrupts the negative behavior. It removes the child from the center of attraction, and it gives the child a chance to calm down.

CONSIDER

Corporal punishment (such as slapping a child's hand or spanking) may stop a misbehavior, but it sends the wrong message. It teaches the child that it is acceptable to use physical violence to force people to do things they don't want to do.

To get the most benefit from a time-out, choose a location that's away from the action to make your child feel somewhat isolated, but close enough for you to keep an eye on her. If your child won't voluntarily go to the time-out chair, lead or carry her to the designated spot. Expect protests and ignore them. Make the child stay in the time-out chair for just a short time (1 minute for each year of age is a good guideline). When the time is up, welcome your child back.

Setting limits is a good first step toward teaching children self-control. But between the ages of 18 and 36 months it won't be enough to end tantrums. The frustration of learning how the world works and not having the cognitive or physical abilities to do everything they would

SCIENCE TO TAKE HOME

There is an established connection between the internalization of a moral voice and the style of discipline parents use. A number of studies on the early development of internalization have shown that 1- and 2-year-olds are more likely to internalize parental directives and follow rules without constant reminders or threats when parents treat them with warmth and sensitivity, explain their rules clearly, and don't rely on physical punishment (Stayton, Hogan, & Salter-Ainsworth, 1971).

like is sometimes just too much for toddlers to bear. Tantrums are inevitable, but the way you respond to them will tell your child a great deal about your disciplinary expectations. Again, being too permissive or too strict leads to more, rather than fewer, tantrums. Your best reaction to an emotional explosion is to neither overreact with anger nor to give in to the child's demands. Instead, talk to him firmly but calmly. Say "You will not get what you want by crying and kicking your feet. When you calm down, we'll talk about your problem." Then create some calming-down time by sending him to his room or to a time-out place, or by ignoring him. This helps a child feel he has some control over the situation, and it keeps his sense of self and competency intact.

Teaching a toddler to behave and show self-control is not easy. It is a very slow and not-so-steady process. The key is to be patient and to never tire of repeating yourself. A toddler's memory is not very good; what you explained last week means nothing this week. Her impulsive nature makes it very difficult to stop misbehaving even when she does remember the rules. That's why you must select a few very important rules and repeat them over and over to help your child eventually learn what's right and what's wrong in the world she lives in.

JUST A PHASE?

On average, toddlers will comply with specific parental commands and requests about two out of three times—even during the "terrible twos." If your toddler has developed a pattern of not complying with or of defying your directive *most* of the time, and this oppositional behavior has persisted for more than 6 months, it's time to seek professional advice.

Parenting to Teach Self-Control

- Use discipline most often to teach and protect rather than to scold and punish.
- As your first line of attack, use disciplinary tactics that avoid conflict.

- Teach your child what she can and can't do by setting limits.
- Make your limits (rules) clear, consistent, and fair.
- Enforce your rules by praising your child for keeping them.
- Use punishment to enforce rules less frequently than you use praise.
- Use the time-out strategy as a consequence for violating the rights of others.
- When your child throws a tantrum, stay calm, remove him from the action, and tell him you will talk about his problem when he calms down.
- When teaching your child self-control, be patient and never tire of repeating yourself.

Avoid

- Using a discipline style that is either too strict or too permissive.
- Using corporal punishment to improve behavior; it often makes matters worse in the long run.
- Making your rules too long or too verbal.
- Changing the rules; be consistent.
- Having too many or inappropriate rules.
- Sending your toddler to the time-out place for more than a minute or two.
- Overreacting to tantrums with anger, but don't give in to tantrums and let the child have her way.
- Expecting that because your child knows something is wrong, he has the impulse control to resist doing it.

REMEMBER

To teach your child self-control, treat him or her with warmth and sensitivity; set limits that are clear, consistent, and fair; and don't rely on physical punishment.

Manners

Two-year-old Joel ran up to the playground slide and pushed his way into the front of the line. "Hey!" yelled little Willy, shoving him out of the way. "You can't cut." Although Joel may not look like he's ready to pass the Miss Manners test, he is now old enough to learn how to be polite. In fact, it's actually easier to teach good manners at this early age than it is to teach them to older children once rude habits have set in. Toddlers are anxious to please and ready to learn how to treat others.

CONSIDER

If you don't teach your toddler the rules of common courtesy, the other kids will. If a child hits a playmate, he'll get hit back. If she grabs a toy, someone will grab it back.

General discussions about good manners won't have much of an impact at this age, so use on-the-spot opportunities. When you see your child cut in line, that's the time to say "Cutting in line makes the other children angry. They won't like you if you don't wait your turn." When your child receives a gift from Grandma, immediately have her say "Thank you." If she makes a mess with her table food, tell her that food is for eating, not playing. If he receives a gift, let him draw a thank-you picture.

You also teach good manners through example. Toddlers live to imitate their parents, so model good manners for them. Speak politely when talking to them. Say "Please come to eat," and "Thank you for picking up your toys." Let your children hear you speak politely to others. Let them see you hold the door for a fellow grocery shopper with a heavy load or hear you say "Excuse me" when you accidentally bump into someone on the street. Children this age are not too young to follow your example; you can expect them to use words like *please*, *thank you*, *excuse me*, and *may I?* You can also help them make the connection between acts of kindness and the appropriate words. Say, for instance, "Mommy did something nice for you just now. I need to hear a 'thank you.' " Or, say "If you want something, I'd like to hear a 'please.' "

Pretend play is a fun way for young children to learn good manners. All the teddy bears at the tea party should be served before the young host. The dolly should have the first ride in the wagon, and then the host can take a turn. Even playing store or restaurant gives children opportunities to practice asking for things politely. Through play, a toddler's civility can grow.

Good manners should be a daily routine, not something put on only in public. By making mannerly behavior and consideration for others part of your family's everyday life, you make it more likely that your children will display these qualities when they're away from home. It makes sense that a child who never says "Thank you" at home is not going to say it to anyone else in the world, either.

When you do go out, anticipate situations that will require good manners and explain in advance your expectations for proper behavior. If you are going to visit a relative's home, for example, you might tell your children in advance, "No running in the house or shouting at the dinner table." But don't overdo it. Remember that toddlers can't remember too many directions at once. Focus on one or two new behaviors at a time. Keep after these until they become automatic; then introduce others.

Manners are taught to little people with lots of patience and repetition. They will not remember how to be polite very often, and they will completely forget everything you've taught them when they are tired or hungry. Despite your best efforts, they will not master the finer points of civility just yet (such as eating with a fork or always using a tissue to wipe their nose). But with persistent guidance, toddlers can learn that manners are all about treating others with respect and kindness–and then, one day when you least expect it, they will be surprisingly polite and considerate.

Parenting to Teach Good Manners

- Use on-the-spot opportunities to teach your child manners.
- Teach good manners through example.
- Use pretend play to teach good manners.
- Anticipate situations that will require good manners and explain in advance your expectations for proper behavior.
- Focus on one or two new rules of etiquette at a time. Keep after these until they become automatic; then introduce others.
- When teaching manners, use lots of patience and repetition.

Avoid

- Thinking your toddler is too young to learn about manners. It's easier to teach good manners at this early age than it is to teach them to older children once rude habits have set in.
- Spending too much time talking about manners. General discussions won't have much of an impact at this age.
- Saving good manners for public show. Make manners a part of your daily routine.
- Overdoing your rules of etiquette. Toddlers can't remember too many directions at once.
- Expecting your toddler to master the finer points of civility just yet.

REMEMBER

Manners are taught to little people with lots of patience and repetition.

36 Months to the Sixth Birthday

STAGE 3

Dear Diary,

Where did my baby go? Christopher just turned 6 years old and he suddenly looks so grown up to me. He has put aside his "baby" toys and now he's a blur on wheels as he zips around on his roller skates and bicycle (with no training wheels!). He seems so much more coordinated and in control of the way he walks and skips and jumps.

He's also gained much better control over his emotions. The temper tantrums of those toddler days are just about completely over. Now when he's really angry he'll often use words to let me know how he feels. I have to admit that it's hard not to laugh when he puts his hands on his hips, pouts up his lips, and very seriously says, "I'm really mad at you."

Christopher uses his imagination in such wonderful ways. Right now he likes to dash around like an action character out of a TV show ready to slay any bad guys who might be stalking our house. He is my protector and my hero. (But he still needs some comforting when the monsters who have taken up residence under his bed threaten to come out at night.) And he creates such wonderful dialogues to go along with the scenes he acts out. In general, his language skills are exceptional, I think. He talks and talks all day long—often to himself when there's nobody else around to listen.

Most of the time, Christopher has plenty of friends to listen to his stories. Ever since he started preschool he has always liked to have friends come over to the house. They don't always get along, and none of them (including Christopher) have the most sophisticated social skills, but they're all learning. Just the other day I heard Christopher ask his friend if he would like something to eat. (It's possible that he himself was hungry and hoped he had a better chance of getting a snack if his friend asked for it, but I like to think he's learning to consider other people's feelings.)

Now that Christopher is in preschool, life around here can get pretty hectic, trying to get everybody out the door on time. We learned a few years ago that things work best for Christopher (and us!) when we keep him on a pretty consistent schedule. He's so familiar with the drill by now that it's been really easy to get him washed up and into bed a night and then up again and out the door in the morning. I can see trouble coming down the road, though. He's starting to complain that his friends are allowed to stay up later and watch more TV than he can. I'm surprised how early peer pressure begins! I'm also surprised how quickly he's picked up stereotypical notions about the differences between girls and boys. For someone who wasn't always sure if he was a boy or a girl two years ago, he certainly has lined up gender differences along a pretty strict line now. When I asked him to put the paper plates on the table the other day, he told me with much conviction that boys don't do chores in the kitchen. Where does he get these ideas??

Most of the time, Christopher is very anxious to help out around the house. He's quite proud when he can vacuum and dust (I'm sure this is just a phase). And he seems very anxious to try anything new and challenging (like pouring his own milk into his cereal bowl). Of course, the more he helps, the more messes I have to clean up, but I'm trying to bite my tongue and let him do things for himself. It makes him so happy to be independent.

Lately, my little boy has turned into a moral dictator. He has very strong opinions about what is right and what is wrong. The rules of the game can't be broken or even bent. The right answer can only be the one he wants it to be. He gets very frustrated if we all don't see things his way. This insistence on seeing and doing things his way has led to quite a few arguments. Sometimes I'm not sure if I should just ignore him and let him think he's in charge or if I should put down my foot and let him know who's boss. I'm finding that the middle ground between these two extremes usually works best. I listen to his feelings and beliefs and then explain my point of view and why sometimes my way is the best way. I'm also noticing that the best way to teach Christopher how to get along is through my own example. When I am kind and considerate to him, he responds the same way. On the other hand, when I'm acting impatient or even rude, he quickly adopts the same manner. It's a tough job being a good parent–but all it takes is a big hug to make it all worthwhile.

Emotional Health

Preschoolers who feel safe and secure in their parents' love are ready to venture away from the emotional security of the home–but not for long. Between the age of 3 years and the sixth birthday, you'll see that your child continues to need your love and affection even though she's not as quick to ask for it. You'll also find that your child is able to show some emotional control; she is more subdued about showing her feelings of great joy and is slowly learning how to manage her strong feelings of anger. This is also the time when fears of things imagined (like monsters and ghosts) accompany the growth of creative and abstract thinking. This is a challenging time for your child, full of emotional ups and downs.

Love and Affection

As preschoolers strive for more independence, their relationship with their parents changes–no longer do they constantly clamor for physical contact. Your preschooler will less frequently pull and tug on and cling to your body. He will spend more time venturing away from you and less time hugging and kissing you. This is a positive sign of development, but like all developmental steps, young children often take two steps forward and an occasional step backward.

The independent 4-year-old who one day suddenly clings to her parent may be considered annoying; the parent will often reject the behavior and push the child away. The rambunctious 5-year-old who generally can't sit still at all, but who one day wants to watch television sitting on his mom's lap, may be told he's too big to sit so close. The 3-year-old who wants to be rocked in the rocking chair like a baby may be reminded that she is no longer an infant. This rejection of physical affection is usually well intentioned, based on the mistaken notion that dependency in preschoolers should be discouraged. True, preschoolers should be spending less and less time attached to their parents, but the

SCIENCE TO TAKE HOME

Secure, closely attached preschoolers have been found to be more capable of relating to their peers than are less secure children. It has been found that preschoolers who failed to form close parental bonds during infancy engaged in a greater number of deviant hostile behaviors in the classroom. And in addition to interacting more successfully with peers, secure children are also more comfortable in interacting with adult strangers (Hughes, Noppe, & Noppe, 1996).

occasional need to be held should not be punished. If children are frustrated in their attempts to obtain nurturance and warmth when they need it, their dependent behavior increases as they try to satisfy their needs. On the other hand, children who receive consistent nurturance feel safe and protected. They venture forth, knowing they have a secure base. Whenever your preschoolers will let you, hug, kiss, and hold them.

Physical affection can become a gender issue at this age. Dads (and sometimes moms) may begin to worry that too much hugging and kissing will turn a boy into a sissy. Concerned about raising "real men," some dads begin withholding their hugs and kisses and replace them with high-fives or a pat on the back. This is a mistake, because one predictor of masculinity in sons is actually the father's warmth and closeness. One way of conveying these feelings is by being physically affectionate. There's never a reason to hold back on hugging and cuddling a preschooler. Boys and girls both need to feel your unrestrained love and affection.

JUST A PHASE?

All preschoolers have moments when they run back to the safety of their parents' arms looking for an extra dose of affection and attention. But if your preschooler spends much more time clinging than exploring, your child may be having trouble separating from you. In this case, seek a professional consultation.

As your preschooler whizzes through the day, seize opportunities to say in small ways, "You're my child and I'm absolutely crazy about you." Give little kisses on top of the head. Give a little pat, and say "I love you." Snuggle often. Find the many simple ways throughout each day to show affection (both physically and verbally) to your child and to admire all your child's positive qualities. Find small ways to say "I love you."

Parenting to Nurture Love and Affection

- Expect your preschooler to spend less time looking for hugs and kisses.

- Expect your preschooler to occasionally regress to a babyish need to cling to you.
- Remember that if children are frustrated in their attempts to obtain nurturance and warmth, their dependent behavior increases.
- Remember that the single best predictor of masculinity in sons is the father's warmth and closeness.
- Seize daily opportunities to say in small ways, "You're my child and I'm absolutely crazy about you."

Avoid

- Pushing your child away when he or she needs extra hugs.
- Buying into the mistaken notion that occasional dependency in preschoolers is related to dependency in adulthood.
- Worrying that too much hugging and kissing will turn a boy into a sissy.
- Holding back on hugging and cuddling a preschooler.

Joy and Anger

The emotions of joy and anger that were so freely and spontaneously displayed in toddlerhood slowly are quieted and restrained during the preschool years. Children between the ages of 3 and 6 become more subdued as they learn to recognize and control their emotions. Spontaneous, open expressiveness starts to become embarrassing and may be considered babyish.

This change in open expression may lead you to think that your child no longer delights in activities that previously sent him into squeals of joy. Now he may calmly watch the seals jump for their food at the zoo, for example, without an outward sign of excitement. Don't assume, however, that he isn't having a great time. A preschooler's increasing verbal abilities may now, more often than hand clapping and squealing, be used to express joy. You may notice that he will now talk a subject to death to express his excitement. Share this new form of communication by engaging in conversations with your child that help him express feelings and emotions. After watching the seals at the zoo, ask him how he feels. Ask him how he thinks the seals feel. Tell him how you feel. Attaching words to feelings helps children

SCIENCE TO TAKE HOME

Discussion of emotions facilitates social sensitivity even in very young children. The authors of one study rated conversations of mothers with their 3-year-old children for discussions of feelings and the variety of emotional themes. The authors measured the children's ability to identify others' emotions at 6½ years. They found that the children who grew up in families that talked about feelings were better at judging the emotions of unfamiliar adults than were children who had not discussed emotions as frequently, regardless of the children's verbal ability and the general frequency of talk in families (Dunn, Brown, & Beardsall, 1991).

gain an understanding of emotions and helps them learn how to control them.

Budding verbal skills also help preschoolers better understand the emotion of anger. The temper tantrums of the toddler years are becoming a thing of the past, but don't let that fool you into thinking you've seen the end of angry outbursts. The preschool years still give kids lots to explode about.

Five-year-old Marissa, for example, was fascinated by her older sister's jigsaw puzzle. But it was a very difficult one. Nothing fit. Suddenly she grabbed a handful of puzzle pieces, pitched them across the room, and let out a howl of disgust. Marissa ran to her room, slamming the door behind her. It might look like Marissa has a trigger temper that should be disciplined, but her actions are merely a sign of frustration that's very common at this age. Children ages 3 to 6 experience great internal turmoil when they get stuck in the gap between their desires and their abilities; this can lead to an outburst because they haven't yet developed the self-control needed to tolerate failure. Their expanding social world contributes to this tension as they begin to compare their capabilities to others': Kate can do this puzzle but I can't; Mary runs faster than I do; Casey can make a block tower, but mine keeps falling down. These comparative situations chip away at a child's budding self-image and fuel angry outbursts.

JUST A PHASE?

If your preschooler has frequent full-blown temper tantrums lasting more than 15 minutes, with kicking, throwing, and screaming, and the child cannot be calmed down by you or other caretakers, it's time for a consultation with a mental health professional. Ask your child's doctor for a referral.

The good news is that 3- to 6-year-olds are ready to learn how to deal with their anger—with a little help from you. Now is a good time to teach your child how to control anger in three steps: (1) accept anger as a natural and normal emotion, (2) verbalize the feeling of anger, and (3) learn to deal with the emotion in acceptable ways. Here's how:

Accept anger as a natural and normal emotion. Children (as well as adults) have a right to be angry. They need to know that feeling angry is not a bad thing and that they should not feel guilty about having this normal emotion. Your goal in teaching a child anger management is not to repress or destroy angry feelings, but rather to help the child accept the feelings and channel them to constructive ends. Strong feelings should not be denied, and angry outbursts should not always be punished. They should be recognized and treated with respect.

One way to respect a child's angry feelings is to try to understand their cause. Anger may be a defense to avoid painful feelings; it may be associated with failure, low self-esteem, and feelings of isolation; or it may be related to anxiety about situations over which the child has no control. Anger may also be associated with sadness. In childhood, anger and sadness are very close to one another, and it is important to remember that much of what an adult experiences as sadness is expressed by a child as anger. Because anger generally has a valid root, it's important to accept anger and work with it, rather than deny and punish it.

Verbalize the feeling of anger. You can help your child learn to talk about the feeling called anger by giving him the words he needs to express himself. When he throws a tantrum because the puzzle pieces won't fit, you might say, "I understand that you're angry because it's hard to do this puzzle." After a few lessons in naming emotions, you might ask your child, "How do you feel right now." When he says, "angry" he's on his way to anger management. You

AGE DIFFERENCES

Three- and four-year-olds are beginning to develop the verbal skills that allow them to express anger in words. It's not until about age 5, however, that a child will be able to consistently verbalize anger. When a favorite toy has been grabbed by another child, for example, a preschooler between the ages of 5 and 6 is likely to skip over the tantrum and articulate his or her feelings to a parent or ask for help in dealing with the situation.

can also teach this lesson through your own example. When you feel yourself getting angry, don't keep it inside or deal with it out of sight. Say to your children, "I'm very angry right now."

Learn to deal with anger in acceptable ways. Verbalizing the feeling called anger is a good first step in anger management, but eventually children must learn how to take action to handle that anger. A parent might say, for example, "Let me tell you what some children would do in a situation like this." Give constructive alternatives to tantrums. Suggest that working together sometimes completes a difficult project, and offer a hand. If your child responds to angry feelings by hitting or pushing, direct your child to hit a designated "anger" pillow. Use your own example, too, to teach anger management skills. When very angry, let your children see that you take deep breaths and slowly count to 10 to calm down. Or, say "I'm going to go to my room for a few minutes to cool off." Following your lead, it won't be long before you hear your child declare "I'm really angry!" as she stomps off to her room. When this happens, you'll know that your child has taken the first giant step toward venting anger in an acceptable manner–a major lesson in the preschool years.

Parenting to Help Children Handle Joy and Anger

- Engage in conversations with your child that help him express feelings and emotions.
- Attach words to feelings to help your child gain an understanding of emotions and help her learn how to control them.

CONSIDER

There is a very thin line at this age between games that are *challenging* and those that are *frustrating.* You can help your preschooler avoid angry outbursts by recognizing the difference. Being in over their heads doesn't promote persistence in children this age; it tends to fuel anger and deflates ambition. Make sure their toys are age-appropriate. Games that require counting or spelling skills your child doesn't yet have aren't enjoyable or educational. Don't challenge preschoolers beyond their capabilities.

- Remember that children ages 3 to 6 experience great internal turmoil when they get stuck in the gap between their desires and their abilities.
- Teach your child how to accept anger as a natural and normal emotion, to verbalize the feeling of anger, and to deal with the emotion in acceptable ways.
- Give your child the words he needs to express strong emotions.
- Teach your child anger management skills through your own example.

Avoid

- Assuming your child isn't having fun when she no longer outwardly expresses spontaneous joy.
- Expecting temper tantrums to end just because your child is out of the "terrible twos."
- Expecting preschoolers to have the self-control needed to tolerate failure.

REMEMBER

Attaching words to feelings help children gain an understanding of emotions and help them learn how to control them.

- Denying or punishing strong feelings. Acknowledge and accept the feeling; focus discipline on unacceptable behaviors.
- Hiding your feelings of great joy or anger. Show your children that these are both normal and natural emotions.
- Frustrating your child by giving him toys that are too challenging and not age-appropriate.

Managing Fear

Infants and toddlers are often afraid of concrete things they can see, like a growling dog or a lightning storm. As the imaginative abilities of preschoolers develop, however, their fears also become more fantastic. Now your child may be afraid not only of the growling dog, but also of the monster under the bed or the burglar who might break into the house–things that cannot be seen, but can be imagined. The preschooler's expanding imagination fuels these fears and magnifies their danger. Although your child requires comfort and help during this time, most children outgrow the fears of their preschool years quite easily with time.

SCIENCE TO TAKE HOME

In a classic study of children's fears reported in 1935, researchers Jersild and Holmes found that younger children are most likely to be afraid of specific things, like strangers, unfamiliar objects, loud noises, or falling. In contrast, children ages 5 to 6 show an increased fear of imaginary or abstract things such as monsters, robbers, the dark, death, being alone, or being ridiculed. Fifty years later, researchers found most of the same fears in preschool children, except that fears of the dark, of being alone, and of strange sights are now appearing at an earlier age (Craig, 1996).

The fears of preschoolers grow from three primary sources:

- *Direct experience.* If your child associates her doctor with a painful inoculation, she may come to fear all doctors. If a child is bitten by a dog, he may grow to be terrified of dogs. These understandable fears can develop when something bad, frightening, or embarrassing happens to a child.
- *The experiences of others.* If your child sees another child cry in pain after falling off a swing set, he may become afraid of swings. If a young child, who cannot yet separate fact from fantasy, watches a frightening television show or movie, she is likely to become fearful. Your own fearful reaction to things such as bugs, deep water, or lightning can teach your child to fear. The ability to empathize with others is a desirable developmental task, but it can also lead children to experience fear based on the experiences of others.
- *The unknown.* Preschoolers know every nook and cranny of their environment. They like the security and comfort of the familiar—they do not usually like new experiences and situations. The unknown pours gasoline on the fires of a young imagination. Anything can happen once a child begins the mental game of "What if. . . ."

With sensitivity, patience, and a bit of creativity, you can help your child handle the normal fears of childhood:

Acknowledge the fear. Try to accept your child's fears and understand their intensity. You will not get rid of them by insisting, "Don't be silly; there's nothing to be afraid of," or "You're acting like a baby; stop being afraid." Instead, acknowledge that the feeling of fear is very real. You might say, "I can see that that clown frightens you."

Talk about the feeling of fear. Tell your child that everyone–including you–is fearful sometimes. Be willing to share your own fears. You might say, "I understand how you feel; I used to be afraid of lightning myself."

Share the feeling. A child who feels afraid almost always feels alone. Read your child books about characters who are afraid of similar things, such as moving to a new home or going to preschool for the first time. Hearing about this shared fear and a character's ability to conquer the fear can help your child develop ways to face her own fears.

Give your child control. If your child feels helpless against an unseen invader, you can use his imagination to give him power over this fear. If there is a monster hiding in the closet, for example, you might give your child a spray bottle of water that has special monster protection powers. Spray the room before bedtime to keep all monsters out. You might also ask your child to draw a picture of the monster; tell him to crumple up the picture and throw it away so the monster can't come around anymore. Post a notice on your child's bedroom door: "No monsters allowed here!"

Reduce exposure to scary things. Knowing your child's imagination is stronger than her sense of reality, limit her exposure to violent and frightening television shows and movies. Make sure shows are age-appropriate before you allow your child to watch. Even the evening news can be too frightening for a preschooler.

Prepare. You can reduce scary experiences by preparing your child in advance for new situations. Before you go to the circus or the dentist, talk to your child about what to expect. If possible, find books and pictures of what he will see. Talk about what he can expect when you get there.

Parenting to Help Children Handle Fear

- Remember that a preschooler's expanding imagination fuels fears and magnifies dangers.
- Talk to your child's doctor about fears that persist for several months and interfere with normal daily living.

- Try to accept your child's fears and understand their intensity.
- Tell your child that everyone–including you–is fearful sometimes.
- Read your child books about characters who are afraid of things.
- Help your child use imagination to gain power over this fear.
- Reduce scary experiences by preparing your child in advance for new situations.

REMEMBER

As the imaginative abilities of preschoolers develop, their fears also become more fantastic. Now your child may be afraid not only of the growling dog, but also of the monster under the bed or the burglar who might break into the house–things that cannot be seen, but can be imagined.

Avoid

- Worrying too much about childhood fears. Most children outgrow the fears of their preschool years quite easily with time.
- Passing on your own fears to your child.
- Downplaying, ridiculing, or criticizing your child's fears.
- Exposing your child to violent and frightening television shows and movies.

Cognitive Development

There is an explosion of cognitive growth between the ages of 3 and 6. Children can now recognize problems and create solutions through newfound problem-solving skills. The development of symbolic thought allows the imagination to expand cognitive powers. And the use of language to explore and ask questions helps children learn about the symbolic and abstract aspects of life. This is an exciting time for the growth of intelligence and a time that opens the door wide to parental influence.

Problem Solving

Preschoolers' ability to solve problems steadily evolves as their thinking skills mature, but the process is slow. You'll notice that your child's solutions will not always seem logical, but that's simply because a child does not think in the same way you do. A few differences include the following:

- *Transductive reasoning.* Preschoolers believe that if *A* causes *B*, then *B* must cause *A*. If you honk the horn, the car will go. If you can make a shadow, the sun will come out.
- *Seriation and classification.* Preschoolers cannot put a series of sticks in order from largest to smallest. Nor can they classify items. When young children are given a number of plastic shapes, including squares, triangles, and circles of different colors, and are asked to put things that are alike into a pile, most children younger than 5 do not organize their choices on any particular logical basis. They may put a red triangle and a blue triangle together, but then throw in a red square (Kaplan, 1991).
- *Conservation.* Preschoolers cannot comprehend that quantities remain the same regardless of changes in their appearance. They cannot see how a tall thin glass and a short fat glass can hold the

same amount of water. They do not believe that a bunch of pennies piled together can be the same number as pennies spread out over a large area. They do not yet understand that a ball of clay that is rolled out into a worm shape still contains the same amount of clay.

- *Appearance versus reality.* Preschoolers base their judgments simply on how things look to them at the present time. Show a 3-year-old a red toy car and cover the car with a green filter that makes it look black. Now hand the car (without the filter) to the child, and then put the car behind the filter again. When you ask the child what color the toy is, the child will say black (Flavell, 1986).
- *Irreversibility.* Preschoolers cannot reverse operations. If a clay ball is rolled into a worm shape in front of them, they cannot mentally rearrange the clay back to its original form. When a preschooler is asked if he has a sister, he may say yes. When asked whether his sister has a brother, he will say no.
- *Egocentrism.* Children see everything from their own viewpoint and are incapable of taking someone else's view into account. This affects their interpretation of their physical and social world. Child developmentalist Piaget showed a model of three mountains to young children and asked them to consider how the display might look to a doll sitting in different positions around the model. The children could not do this accurately. Preschoolers reason that everyone sees the world as they do.
- *Animism.* Young preschoolers believe that everything is capable of being conscious and alive. Stuffed animals have feelings. A book that falls off the shelf can be scolded. A balloon that flies away wanted to be free. This belief becomes less evident when children reach the age of 4 or 5.

CONSIDER

Preschool children do not all progress intellectually at the same pace. You should not be frightened if your child is not counting to 10 by age 3 or reading books by age 6. Some children put more of their attention and energy into other kinds of intelligence, such as making friends or accomplishing athletic feats. Early achievement does not necessarily signal superior intelligence, just as delayed achievement does not necessarily signal a future deficit in intellect.

Despite certain limitations in thinking skills, your preschooler is always exploring, listening, doing, and learning how the world works. You can give your child a hand by continuing to practice divergent thinking skills (creating a variety of alternative solutions) in real-life situations. For example, you might ask your child to think of many different ways to respond when another child takes away a toy. Don't judge these solutions as right or wrong–go for quantity first. Maybe your child will suggest: Grab it back. Threaten the other person. Ask for it. Tell the teacher. Cry. All of these show divergent thinking.

Next, help your child practice the skill of consequential thinking to evaluate those solutions. For example, the child whose toy was taken by another can be guided to think, "If I grab it back, then she will hit me. If I tell the teacher, she will tell me to solve the problem myself. If I cry, I won't get the toy back." This kind of thinking helps children solve problems constructively. (See Stage 4 for information about a formal problem-solving program using these skills.)

There are two rules you should remember when promoting problem-solving skills in preschoolers:

Don't solve all your child's problems. If he can't get his shoe on, make a suggestion about how it might be done, but don't kneel down and do it yourself. If he can't find a toy, don't search for it yourself; instead, suggest places where your child might find it. Give lots of opportunities for your child to feel the pride of solving his own problems.

Ask lots of questions. When your child is facing a problem, ask questions that will help her find her own solution. When she cries because the glue won't stick, don't rush in with the solution; ask questions such as "What do you think would happen if you used

---

SCIENCE TO TAKE HOME

Puppets are an effective tool for teaching social problem-solving skills. Puppet presentations can nurture a sensitivity to personal and interpersonal problems by portraying a particular social difficulty that is relevant to young children. Children are not born with an understanding of social interaction—they must learn how to identify and resolve the variety of possible problems that can arise over the course of human relationships. Puppet shows can be used to dramatize social situations and present constructive solutions (Smith, 1979).

---

more glue?" or "Do you think it will stick better if you give it time to dry?" Also, use questions to pass the time and start conversations. Ask your child questions such as "How can we tell if the wind is blowing?" or "Where do butterflies go in the winter?" There are no right or wrong answers here; just lots of fun brainstorming.

Parenting to Build Problem-Solving Skills

- Remember that your child does not think about things the same way you do.
- Expect your child to consider only those solutions that fit his own point of view.
- Practice divergent thinking skills by asking your child to think of many possible solutions to her daily problems.
- Help your child practice the skill of consequential thinking by asking what would happen if he acted out one of his suggested solutions.
- Use puppets to help your child see how others solve the kinds of problems she faces.
- Ask questions that will help your child find his own solutions.

REMEMBER

Despite certain limitations in thinking skills, your preschooler is always exploring, listening, doing, and learning how the world works. You can give your child a hand by helping him or her practice divergent and consequential thinking skills.

Avoid

- Judging your child's thinking skills based on your own sense of logic.
- Asking your child to consider another's point of view when solving problems–he can't.
- Solving all your child's problems for her.
- Answering all your child's questions without first asking him what he thinks might be the answer.
- Evaluating a child's answer as right or wrong

Play and Imagination

Four-year-old Joshua never told a small tale where a big one would do. "It's true!" he'd swear. "I ate ten pizza pies all by myself at Joey's party, and then I had fifty bowls of ice cream." His parents were upset by this insistence on stretching the truth, but the more they insisted that he tell what really happened, the bigger the stories became. "And then a big, green ugly monster jumped out of the bush and grabbed me!"

A child's imagination can set parents to wondering what's normal, healthy fun and what's negative or abnormal behavior. What is the difference between exaggerating and lying? These kinds of worries feed the dilemma of whether to encourage imaginative play or keep it reined in.

Rest assured that fantasy is a normal and integral part of cognitive development. Unfortunately, in our fast-paced, high-tech world, where achievement and success are so highly valued, a child's need to pretend is often ignored or even discouraged. This is a shame, because fantasy stimulates a child's imagination, creativity, and problem-solving abilities. In fact, it has been found that children with a high level of fantasizing tend to be better at concentrating on tasks, to have more self-control, and to be able to come up with new, rather than stereotyped, responses to problems. You can encourage your child's cognitive, social, and emotional skills by accepting imaginative play as normal and useful and by encouraging opportunities for its growth.

CONSIDER

A combination of refined motor skills and increased cognitive sophistication means that preschoolers love many old-fashioned toys such as wooden building blocks, Play-Doh, finger paints, dolls, and dress-up clothes.

Like Josh, most children in this age group love to tell tall tales. They use their stories to attract attention and to surround themselves with a measure of glory. Often, like Joshua, many get carried away and forget the actual facts of an event. Their exaggeration is sometimes due to a loss of cognitive control over facts, and they actually are unaware that they are being untruthful. The difference between reality and fantasy still isn't firmly established for these children, so their fibs can't be considered *dishonesty* in the adult sense of the word.

You shouldn't worry too much about these childish departures from fact. If your child is especially inclined to tell tall tales, harsh punishments are not appropriate. Instead, give your child a gentle dose of *reality feedback*. When your 3-year-old comes back from the zoo and tells you he swam with the seals, don't accuse him of lying. Instead, you might say, "Well, that's a good story. It sounds like you really like the seals. Tell me what they looked like and what they did."

AGE DIFFERENCES

At age 3, children can rarely distinguish between reality and fantasy. By age 6 they have a much better understanding of the difference, but may still occasionally blur the lines.

This fertile time for imaginary play also encourages the continued fun of role-playing. But now, instead of imitating the people they see daily (as children under age 3 do), chil-

SCIENCE TO TAKE HOME

In her book *Failure to Connect: How Computers Affect Our Children's Minds, for Better and Worse,* educational psychologist Jane M. Healy proposes the controversial point of view that children under age 7 should not be allowed access to a computer. Among her reasons for this stand is the belief that computers take kids away from peer play, which is so vital to social development and imagination. Also, Healy believes the computer gives the child someone else's visual images at precisely the time when children need to be developing their own image-making capacities. This is certainly something to think about (Healy, 1998).

dren ages 3 to 6 begin to take on the mask of the many adults who live in the world. Children now pretend to be grown up: Police, firefighters, pirates, pilots, teachers, and doctors run around the house in all manner of costumes. Also popular are fictional characters from books, movies, or television. Children love to construct action plans that mimic the story lines they hear and see. One of the most common themes of their imaginary play involves averting threats. Children will often pretend they must conquer a monster or a bad guy. By trying on these different roles, children learn to solve problems through experimentation, and they learn how to express emotions, worries, and wishes. This gives them a sense of power and control that they lack in their daily interactions with adults.

Often, preschoolers' pretend games become quite aggressive, and it's natural to wonder if violent television shows may be responsible. Although violent programming has been found to have a negative impact on some young children, in truth, violence has been characteristic of the play and storytelling of 3- to 6-year-olds since long before the advent of movies or television. These children love to tell stories that are loaded with all sorts of large-scale, high-impact, and often extremely unpleasant events—probably because it makes for good drama. Violent tales and adventures also help children work out their instinctual aggression. Getting these impulses out in the open gives them a feeling of mastery and personal control. As long as your child isn't aggressive with peers and family, there's no need to worry if some fantasy play involves themes of violence.

JUST A PHASE?

A preschooler's complete lack of interest in pretend play may be a sign of a serious problem such as depression or autism. Consult your pediatrician or a child psychologist.

Parenting to Encourage Play and Imagination

- Remember that fantasy is a normal and integral part of cognitive development.
- Foster imagination by offering lots of creative materials such as clay, finger paints, and blocks.
- Keep in mind that the difference between reality and fantasy still isn't firmly established for all preschoolers, so their fibs can't be considered *dishonesty* in the adult sense of the word.
- Encourage your child's love of role-playing.
- Remember that violent themes in imaginary play can help children work out their instinctual aggression.

Avoid

- Issuing harsh punishments when your child tells tall tales.
- Expecting your child to be able to distinguish between reality and fantasy.
- Allowing preschoolers excessive exposure to computer games.
- Taking the lead when you role-play games with your child. Be a follower and let your child tell you who you should pretend to be. Ask for direction and guidance about what you should do or say.
- Insisting, "That could never happen" when you hear yet another of the illogical story lines your child loves to tell. Let your child imagine without fear of upsetting your logical view of things.

REMEMBER

It has been found that children with a high level of fantasizing tend to be better at concentrating on tasks, to have more self-control, and to be able to come up with new, rather than stereotyped, responses to problems. These are all positive characteristics that you can promote in your child by accepting imaginative play as normal and useful and by encouraging opportunities for its growth.

Language Development

Five-year-old Leigha concentrated with all her might as she "read" her book aloud to her mother. Her little fingers pointed to each word as she read the story from start to finish, leaving out not a single detail. Although the words coming from her mouth did not match the words written on the pages of the book, Leigha was using very complex thinking skills. She had learned that each group of symbols represented a word. She knew the story unfolded from the front to the back of the book and that the logic of the words progressed from left to right. This simple act of pretend reading is a wonderful accomplishment that illustrates how the development of language skills between ages 3 and 6 is the foundation on which intelligence grows.

The cognitive skills of 3- to 6-year-old children are most obvious in their rapidly expanding vocabulary. These children can now describe what they see and feel. They can remember and retell parts of a story they've heard. They can use language to work out ways to share and solve problems. Language development teaches children to think symbolically as they learn that words represent objects and abstract ideas. This knowledge opens up a whole new world.

There are many signs of language development you can watch for at this time:

- *Self-talk.* Your preschooler will spend a good deal of time talking to herself. She will tell herself what she is doing, command and criticize herself, and repeat parental prohibitions and encouragements. This is her way of practicing verbal communication.
- *Tenses.* To a toddler, all things happen in the present. A preschooler will begin to use the future and then the past tense in his communications. Words like *tomorrow, later,* and *yesterday* begin to be understood.

SCIENCE TO TAKE HOME

In the study "Reading to Pre-schoolers Exposed: Is the Emperor Really Naked?" it was found that interaction during story time between a parent and a preschool child can be a predictor of future academic success. Parents were studied who not only read books to their children, but also went beyond the text to ask questions and make commentaries that led their children into more abstract thinking and linguistic expression. The children were asked how and why events took place in stories and were encouraged to make comments about unfolding events and relate them to past experiences in their lives. Unlike children who did not experience this interactive reading, these children not only successfully learned to read in the early elementary years, but were also successful in "reading to learn" in the middle elementary years (Lonigan, 1994).

- *Pronouns.* As a toddler, your child practiced using the pronouns *me* and *mine.* Now your child is becoming familiar with other pronouns, such as *he, she,* and *them.*
- *Differentiation.* In the past, the word *daddy* applied to any grown-up male. A preschooler, however, will learn to distinguish between *Daddy,* who lives at home, and *daddies,* who live in other children's homes.

Language development progresses on an individual schedule that varies from child to child. In general, however, you may see your child's language progress in these stages:

- *Age 3.* The child uses up to 900 words, and sentences average 3 to 4 words.
- *Age 4.* The child uses up to 1,500 words, and sentences average about 5 words. The child also uses more complex grammar in sentences, saying things like, "Daddy drives in the car."
- *Age 5.* The child uses up to 2,000 words, and sentences average 6 words. The child uses language to explore by asking questions like, "What is this for?" and "How does this work?"
- *Age 6.* The child uses about 2,500 words, and sentences average 7 words. The child can sustain a focused conversation.

JUST A PHASE?

You might begin to suspect that your child is not progressing intellectually at age 3 if he or she is not yet talking in three-word phrases with pronunciation that can be understood by a stranger. Once a child enters preschool or kindergarten, your child's teacher can tell you if there seems to be a learning problem. Indicators in preschool might include the child's inability to follow simple directions or to listen carefully and repeat basic information. In kindergarten, children should be able to grasp the concepts of letters and numbers. If you or the teacher suspect a problem in cognitive development, ask for a child-study team evaluation by school personnel that will include intelligence testing. The earlier a problem is detected, the sooner remedial work can begin.

Parenting to Encourage Language Development

- Talk with and listen to your child. Really pay attention and converse. Get down on your child's level. Maintain eye contact. Be patient with the child's halting speech pattern. Let the child talk without interruption or correction.
- Recognize that self-talk is a positive developmental step.
- Read to your child. Oral reading teaches not only about the sounds of words, but about cause and effect, about problem solving and consequences, about personality types, and about the order of sequence.
- When you read to your child, make time for questions and answers. Stop in the middle, for example, and ask your child "What do you think will happen next?"

Avoid

- Correcting your child's mistakes or expecting her to stick to the written word when she tries to "read" to you. Just enjoy the retelling of the story based on memory and pictures.
- Hesitating to get a professional evaluation for a preschooler who can't follow simple directions or listen carefully and repeat basic information.
- Interrupting or correcting your child when he makes a grammatical mistake. Instead, simply repeat the thought using correct language. Turn "I goed home" into "Yes, I know you went home."

REMEMBER

The development of language skills between ages 3 and 6 is the foundation on which intelligence grows.

Family and Peer Relationships

Preschoolers are ready to reach out beyond their family and become part of the world around them. They like to be with friends, and they need lots of playtime experiences to practice the give-and-take of social relationships. With so much to do and so much to learn, these children are often emotionally worn out at the end of the day—but whining, dawdling, and crying can be reduced if their days can be scheduled around a predictable routine. The security of knowing what to expect next gives them a feeling of control that comes in handy as peer pressure to conform now begins in earnest.

Building Friendships

Five-year-old Charles begged his dad, "Please? Can Ronnie come over to play?" Charles's dad hesitated. "Charles spends all week in school with his friends," he says, "Why does he have to have them come over to our house on weekends?" You can bet that children this age will nag to have certain friends visit their homes on a play date for very good reasons. At home, the time is unstructured, the rules are up for grabs, the toys and games are personal favorites, the task of sharing becomes an intimate choice, and the fun of laughing, running, and being silly isn't prohibited. And if all that isn't enough reason, add this: The single best childhood predictor of adult adaptation is not school grades, and not classroom behavior, but rather the adequacy with which the child gets along with other children (Hartup & Moore, 1990). It appears that the groundwork for the ability to make and sustain friendships is laid very early in life—and is made firm with the help of parental support and supervision.

There's no doubt that children first learn about friendship from their parents. Right from the start the development of social competence relies on having warm, supportive, and encouraging parents to whom a baby feels deeply and affectionately attached. The security of this

SCIENCE TO TAKE HOME

Children who are rejected by their peers often have mothers who are less likely to teach them about social skills, who spend less time in child-centered activities, and who use more punishment and less reasoning and explanation in discipline. Fathers of rejected children are also reported to be less likely to spend time in child-centered activities (Kennedy, 1992).

attachment allows the preschooler to reach out to others for companionship and enjoyment. Next, children learn about relationship building from what they observe in their environment. Traits that build or destroy relationships include warmth and hostility, trust and mistrust, friendliness and anger, and give-and-take and selfishness. If you want your child to be a good friend to other children, model friendly behaviors among your own family members. It's a fact that well-liked kids are cooperative, outgoing, and fair. Most kids learn these traits through the example of their parents.

Along with your good example, children need opportunities to practice what they've learned. This is where play dates come in. Studies have shown that peer acceptance in the preschool is related to the extent to which parents initiate play opportunities for their children and supervise those get-togethers. This makes sense because children who have difficulty making friends become excluded from social activities, and thus have less experience and fewer opportunities to develop, learn, practice, and refine the skills they lack. Children need guidance to develop the social skills they need to interact with other children.

To organize play dates that help children learn how to become friends, try the following tips:

- Bring out toys that encourage cooperative play, such as puppets or a pet hamster that can be stroked and held by both kids. Don't have

---

AGE DIFFERENCES

- **Three-year-olds typically engage in independent and parallel play, which does not include the acknowledgment or involvement of others.**
- **Four-year-olds still engage in independent and parallel play and will now begin a play style called *complementary structure*, in which there is some degree of cooperation, but the roles of the children are still enacted independently of each other.**
- **Five- and six-year-olds are ready for interactive play. They now focus on how their companions behave, and they continually influence each other during the course of play.**

---

too many toys available, however, since this encourages the children to focus on the toys rather than on each other.

- Allow for some noisy fun. Children should be allowed to be themselves–loud and silly.
- If your child is misbehaving in front of the other kids, call your child over in private and explain the problem and the consequences if the behavior continues. This avoids embarrassing your child in public.
- If a visiting friend is aggressive, firmly explain the rules of the house. End the play date if the friend continues to be aggressive. Your child must feel safe from physical attack.
- If your child cries when the play date is over, set a time limit as the play date begins. Use a timer or a cardboard clock to show when the date will end. It is easier to adjust to time limits that are predictable and certain.
- If your child doesn't want to invite a particular friend over any more, respect your child's right to choose his or her own friends. Children in this stage will tell you whom they want to play with. They will generally pick friends comparable to themselves in age, gender, verbal skills, interests, and athletic ability. They may also exclude those who aren't a perfect match. Three- to six-year-olds like the idea of having a best friend, but your child's best friend can change several times in one day.
- If you don't like the playmate your child is eager to invite over because you believe the playmate is a bad influence, explain your feelings to your child. Plant the seed that this person is not the best playmate to choose. Children need to learn how to identify desirable character traits and behaviors.

When your child's friends have gone home, take some time to talk to your child about the play date. This is the perfect time to coach social skills, using what happened during the play date for concrete examples. If a friend was bossy, tell your child exactly how to insist on one's rights. If the date was boring, help your child figure out why and how to make it more exciting next time. If the children became too rambunctious, encourage your child to think of some quiet play activities. This kind of social discussion will help your child learn how to be a good friend.

JUST A PHASE?

Is your child shy and slow to make friends? This may be a stage the child will grow out of, or it may be the child's personality and something he or she will live with and learn to adjust to as time goes on. In either case, if a shy child is being bullied or excluded from play, it's time to teach some assertiveness skills. Take the role of the other child and play out a typical scene. Help your child practice saying "I'm allowed to play here, too," or "I want to play the grown-up this time."

Parenting to Help Children Develop Friendships

- Be a warm, supportive, and encouraging parent who is well attached to your child.
- Model friendly behaviors among your own family members.
- Initiate play opportunities for your child.
- Remember that children need guidance to develop the social skills they need to interact with other children.

Avoid

- Expecting preschool to supply your child with adequate play time.
- Assuming social skills are learned without your help.
- Showing your child hostility, mistrust, anger, and selfishness at home.
- Limiting play opportunities for a child who has difficulty making friends.
- Ignoring play date problems. Use them to help your child learn how to be a good friend.

REMEMBER

The groundwork for the ability to make and sustain friendships is laid very early in life—and is made firm with the help of parental support and supervision.

Family Rituals and Routines

Three-year-old Trisha was dancing to her favorite music video when her mom announced it was bathtime. "No!" screamed Trisha, setting off one of her all-too-common tantrums. "I won't! I won't!" Trisha isn't being intentionally stubborn or fresh. She's just having a hard time making the transition from one activity to another. What she needs is a routine—something that will reduce the occurrence of random chaos in her day and give her a place in the family that is secure and predictable.

Try to imagine living through a day without being able to tell time and not knowing from one minute to the next what's going to happen. Living like this creates a lot of tension and uncertainty–certainly enough to fuel occasional tantrums when, once again, an activity is interrupted and another is begun without warning. This is how your child spends each day unless there is some kind of routine your child can use to gauge the passage of time. Try to map out a simple schedule that lets your child know when the very basics will happen. Waking, eating, playing, resting, bathing, and sleeping times should be somewhat predictable from one day to the next. They should offer a regularity and rhythm that is soothing and reassuring. This kind of daily routine will reduce behavior problems (such as whining, tantrums, and dawdling) that fuel common daily arguments between parents and preschoolers at these times of the day:

- *Morning time.* A fixed wake-up time is very important in order to establish a child's biological clock so that the child will feel sleepy at the same time each evening. Once that's established, in theory, the morning routine should be very simple: Wake up, wash, dress, eat, and go. So why is it so difficult to get preschoolers out the door? Usually the delay occurs because between each one of these basic steps lies watching television, playing, arguing with siblings, and simple dilly-dallying. Routines to the rescue. It will take time for your child to get into the swing of things, but if you consistently move your child from one event to the next in the same order, at the same time every day, you'll soon be surprised to see your preschooler following the routine without nagging reminders.
- *Before dinner time.* The time while you're preparing dinner can be especially tough on preschoolers. They're tired, they're hungry, and they want your attention. If your child often acts up during this time, schedule a routine quiet activity that your child can count on every day. This might be the time to watch a favorite videotape or television program. This might be a good time for resting on the couch with favorite storybooks. You might make a routine of setting out the coloring books at this time. Whatever it is, do it every day so your child knows that this is what to do while you're making dinner.

- *Dinner time.* Getting kids to come to the table and then sit still during dinner can also be difficult, especially if sometimes they can grab a bite and run, other times they must sit through the whole meal, and still other times they eat in the living room watching television. Set up a routine and stick to it. Some families map out each step: Wash hands, sit at the table, eat dinner, stay until given permission to leave, and bring dishes to the sink. There's nothing to argue about when everybody knows the rules.

- *Bedtime.* What time does your child go to bed? You should be able to say a definite time and stick to it every night. Although there is no absolutely correct bedtime hour, children between the ages of 3 and 6 generally require 10 to 12 hours of sleep a night. Although they will initially complain and protest a nonnegotiable bedtime, children eventually fall into the routine without complaint (if you're consistent and don't give in to their pleas to stay up later once in a while). In our book *Winning Bedtime Battles* (Schaefer & DiGeronimo, 1992), we outline a bedtime routine that follows four steps:

  Step 1: Enforce quiet time. Reserve the hour before bedtime for quiet play. This will lower your children's activity level and prepare their nervous systems for relaxation.

  Step 2: Give advance notice. One-half hour before you want your children to begin getting ready for bed, announce, "A half hour till bedtime." Ten minutes before bedtime, give another warning. This gives children the opportunity to mentally prepare for the switch from awake to sleep time and also to finish whatever activity they're engaged in. When the time is up, use an impersonal, third-party timer like a stovetop buzzer, a kitchen timer, or even a clock radio to signal the end of playtime.

  Step 3: Escort your children to bed. If you yell over the top of your newspaper, "Go brush your teeth and go to bed," you're going to have trouble. But if you get up and escort your children to the bathroom and then to the bedroom, they'll know you mean business (and they won't feel that you're sending them off so you can do wonderful things without them). Putting your children to bed also gives you the opportunity to enjoy a bedtime ritual that will comfort your children. A storybook, a song, and/or a tuck-me-in kiss all ease the transition between wakefulness and sleep.

Step 4: Leave the room. After you've completed your bedtime ritual, don't linger in your child's bedroom. Say a firm "Good night," and leave the room. Any hesitation on your part will be picked up by your children as a possible indication that maybe you really aren't serious about this definite bedtime. If your children cry and beg you not to leave, assure them that you'll set the kitchen timer for 5 minutes and will return when it sounds for another quick kiss.

SCIENCE TO TAKE HOME

Getting your child on a predictable and consistent bedtime schedule may be good for you, too. Researchers have found that improving a child's sleep patterns can also improve the mother's emotional state, along with her perceived control of her child's behavior (Pritchard & Appleton, 1988).

If problems in moving from one activity to another persist, you may want to introduce a reward system to move your child easily through the routine. Depending on what motivates your child, you might say:

- "If you dress, wash, and eat breakfast before eight o'clock, you can watch twenty minutes of TV before we leave for preschool. But no TV watching at all until then."
- "If you wash up, sit at the dinner table, eat your food, and clear the dishes away from your place, you can have dessert. If you skip any one of those steps, you cannot have dessert."
- "If you are in bed by eight o'clock, I'll give you a package of stickers." Or, "If you go to bed on time without complaining every night this week, you can have a friend sleep over on Friday night."

The best kind of reward is obviously something your child likes, but it shouldn't cost you a fortune. Small items that show you're aware of your child's likes and interests should do the trick. You might also try a surprise grab bag. Fill a bag with small inexpensive items that your children like, and let them close their eyes and draw one out each night after they've completed their bedtime routine on time and have said "Good night" without complaint.

CONSIDER

Children who have trouble adapting to change, regulating their feelings, or coping with uncertainty seem to settle down in orderly, routinized environments. Some of these children seem drawn to stimulation, but once they get it, they lose control and act out. Anxious, introverted children may withdraw in tears. These are the children who especially need the world to offer some certainty.

Although establishing family routines requires a bit of forethought and planning on your part, they help children in many ways:

- They give a feeling of empowerment by letting children know what to expect next.
- They ease children's natural feelings of vulnerability by giving order to their world.
- They help children manage impulsive behavior by assuring them of what they're supposed to do next.
- The repetitious aspect of routines helps children develop the habit of self-discipline they need to become self-reliant.

Parenting to Create Rituals and Routines

- Map out a simple schedule that lets your child know when the very basics will happen.
- To get your child out the door on time each day without a tantrum, consistently move her from one event to the next in the same order, at the same time every day.
- If the time before dinner is difficult for your child, schedule a quiet activity that will amuse him while you are busy.
- Be consistent about the behavior you expect at the dinner table.
- Help your child make the transition from wakefulness to sleep with a fixed bedtime and a consistently enforced bedtime routine that allows time for winding down and nightly goodnight rituals.
- Help your child follow a daily routine by offering small rewards. A sheet of stickers is usually enough to motivate preschoolers to get to bed on time.

Avoid

- Chaotic schedules, which tend to promote whining, dawdling, and tantrums.
- Inconsistent schedules that make it difficult for preschoolers to know what's expected of them.
- Eating dinner on the run. Try to maintain a fairly consistent dinner routine so your child has an anchor at the end of the day.

- Sending your child to bed without a personal escort. Tucking your child in lets her know you mean business and it also gives you a special time at the end of the day to let your child know she is safe and loved.

REMEMBER

Waking, eating, playing, resting, bathing, and sleeping times should be consistent and predictable from one day to the next. They should offer a regularity and rhythm that is soothing and reassuring.

Peer Pressure

"You can't be my friend if you play with Amy," said 5-year-old Kristen. Little Maddie felt confused. She wanted to be friends with Kristen, but she wanted to play with Amy, too. Not knowing what to do, Maddie started to cry. How could she stay friends with both girls and not make anyone mad? The peer pressure of friendship had begun.

This kind of pressure is more typical than terrible in this age group. Between the ages of 3 and 6, the traditional signs of real peer pressure begin as children move outside the safe haven of their families into a bigger world of preschool and their first real friendships. It is the pressures and pleasures of these experiences that help children figure out who they are and where they fit into their expanded universe.

CONSIDER

Children who do not have a close relationship with their parents are more vulnerable to negative peer influence.

Watch for the influence of peer pressure on the playground. On any given day, you'll undoubtedly see children copying the play styles of other children. One child will ride down the slide backward, and so will the child who follows him. One will take off her shoes in the sandbox, and suddenly everyone's shoes are off. You'll even see that if a child is excluded from play by one playmate, the others may also exclude that child. Life can be tough when the pressure to conform kicks in.

CONSIDER

You can help your child handle peer pressure by planning ahead:

- **Play what-if games. Occasionally ask your child questions like, "What if Jimmy sees his friend Billy playing in the middle of the street? Should he play in the street, too?"**
- **Talk about problem situations before they happen. Explain to your child, for example, that even if everyone else is riding in the car without a seatbelt, she must still wear hers.**

As you watch your young children copy their friends and perhaps pick up a few bad habits, remember that peer pressure isn't all bad. Although we would all like our children to be independent thinkers and to resist the pull of the crowd, the need to conform grows from a normal and healthy need to be socially connected to others. From cradle to grave we learn how to be socially compatible by finding ways we are alike and different from those around us. This influence will come from many sources.

In addition to playmates, you'll see that siblings are a strong influence on each other. A child will spend twice as much time in the company of siblings as with parents by the time of entering kindergarten. No wonder there's peer influence! The influence often depends on the birth order. In most cases, the older siblings clearly dominate the younger ones. The older children initiate more prosocial and combative behaviors, and the young children imitate more. Sometimes you will see an older child play with a toy and leave it; the younger child will pick up the toy and imitate the older child's play. The older child asserts peer pressure through simple example.

Another source of social influence at this age is the television. Children under the age of 5 watch an average of 25½ hours of television per week (Hughes, Noppe, & Noppe, 1996) and are exposed to about 20,000 commercials a year (Kaplan, 1991). This is where they learn a lot about how to fit into their society. Commercials especially have a lot to say about gender-appropriate forms of play. Watch a few ads for dolls–you'll see no male children anywhere near the toy. Watch a few for weapons, construction toys, or sports equipment–you'll see that

SCIENCE TO TAKE HOME

Peers often serve as enforcers of society's sex-role standards. Researchers watched over 200 preschoolers at play and found marked reactions from peers when children violated appropriate sex-typical behavior patterns. Boys who play with dolls rather than trucks have a tough time: They are criticized five to six times more often by their classmates than are more conforming children. On the other hand, girls who would rather play firefighter than nurse are not treated as harshly; instead, they are ignored and not criticized. Other studies have found that negative peer pressure is an effective way to stop children's cross-sex activity (Hetherington & Parke, 1986).

girls are nowhere to be found. This observation has been the subject of several research studies. All come to the same conclusion: Television ads tell our children how to be a boy and how to be a girl. Stereotyped characters and actions on television shows are also remarkably consistent. Your children will see males engage in more activities and be more aggressive and constructive than females. They will see males portrayed in professional roles and females portrayed as nonprofessionals (usually as family figures). In fact, women are often portrayed as damsels in distress, helpless and victimized until a brave hero rescues them (Hughes, Noppe, & Noppe, 1996). If you wonder why your little daughter "naturally" gravitates to "female" toys like baby carriages and role-plays the mommy, or why your young son is into domineering beat-'em-up action games, take a close look at the television shows and commercials they watch. They are this generation's most persistent form of peer pressure.

At this age, children are open to the influence of others–that's part of growing up. But as the media, other children, and siblings try to influence your child's choices and behaviors, what *you* believe should be explained loud and clear, as well. When the crowd excludes a playmate, take your child aside and explain that doing this hurts the other child's feelings. When a playmate yells, "If you don't do this, I'll never be your friend again," help your child understand that this is not really true, that it is only a tactic used by many people to get their own way. When a friend takes off his shoes in the sandbox, tell your child that she has a choice of whether she wants to do the same. When a television show portrays a woman as dumb or a man as domineering, comment on the fact that not all men and women are like that. Help your child learn that television is not the real world (something that is very difficult for preschoolers to understand). These kinds of simple lessons

---

JUST A PHASE?

Is your child the class bully? Without help and guidance, a child with social problems in preschool is likely to continue having these problems through adulthood. A child who bullies others needs to learn that this kind of behavior is not allowed. Make it clear, "You can't boss other children around." Then teach empathy. Ask your child, "How would you feel if someone said that to you?" This isn't a rhetorical question–wait for an answer. Help your child to understand how the things one says and does affect others.

---

taught on the spot will begin to build the foundation that your children will stand on when they need to resist negative peer pressure in the years ahead.

Parenting to Help Children Deal with Peer Pressure

- Establishing a close relationship with your child will help him be less vulnerable to negative peer pressure.
- Keep in mind that all peer pressure isn't bad.
- Help your older child learn to be a good role model for a younger sibling.
- Monitor television viewing so you can add your own beliefs about gender roles and actions.
- To balance the messages your child receives from friends, siblings, and the media, explain what you believe loud and clear, as well.

REMEMBER

Between the ages of 3 and 6, the traditional signs of real peer pressure begin as children move outside the safe haven of their families into a bigger world of preschool and their first real friendships.

Avoid

- Expecting your child to resist all peer pressure.
- Excessive television exposure.
- Letting your child be pushed into doing things she doesn't want to. Remind her she has a choice about what she chooses to do.

Personal Growth

Preschoolers ages 3 to 6 spend a great deal of their time and energy finding themselves. As they venture away from home they explore their world, their peers, and adults outside their family to find out just how they personally fit into the big picture. This exploration gives them a broader sense of self than they previously understood. Most preschoolers are ready to aim high (sometimes too high) as they set out to do things for themselves and find out how to master and control their environment. They also are ready to take on the responsibility of daily chores that give them a sense of competence and accomplishment.

Sense of Self

As preschoolers observe and experience the world, their sense of who they are begins to broaden. If you say to a young preschooler, "Tell me about yourself," she will respond by describing who she is in terms of one of four characteristics:

- *Physical attributes.* "I have curly hair."
- *Possessions.* "I have a dog."
- *Preferred activities.* "I like to swim."
- *Overt behaviors.* "I can run fast."

Eventually, a preschooler's sense of self expands as she begins to evaluate herself by comparison with others. She will realize, "I am taller than John; Mary can run faster than me; Kurt has a big ball and I have a small ball." Sometimes this ability to compare builds up a child's sense of self ("I'm the only one in my group who knows my colors"). But other times comparisons can diminish budding self-esteem ("I can't draw nice pictures like Ben"). Both are part of the process of building a personal identity. This is also the time when children realize that the world looks different from different viewpoints, and their self-image changes based on what others think of them. Sue can imagine that Billy will think she is mean if she grabs his toy. Kenny knows his mother will think he is a good boy if he cleans up his toys. Personal comparisons and changing viewpoints help children visualize where they fit into their world.

Teachers and peers now have a notable influence on your child's sense of who he is, but your influence is still the strongest. You have many opportunities to make your child feel good about himself and thus boost his self-image. You can help him feel more capable by simply displaying his work and projects around your house. You show him that he is special when you listen to his stories and when you celebrate his successes. You teach him that he is worthy when you value his abilities (by pointing out an area of strength) and his admirable personality traits (by acknowledging when he is kind and thoughtful). You also give him a sense of power and mastery when you allow him to take on the responsibility to make decisions and contribute to the family (by doing chores, for example). Every time your child feels good about himself, it gives a boost to his positive self-identity.

The challenge in building up a child's self-image is to do it without overdoing the praise and giving the child an unrealistic self-picture. As peer comparisons begin, your child will notice that she's not always the best at everything. It's not necessary to convince her that she really is—far better to convince her that she doesn't have to be perfect to feel good about herself. If your child complains that Mary runs faster than she does, don't deny it, or make excuses for your child, or insist that your child practice running so she can beat Mary next time. Instead, offer empathy and then emphasize one of your child's strengths: "You're right. Mary is a very fast runner. But you are much better than Mary at coloring." This helps your child realize that we all have things we're good at and things we're not so good at.

CONSIDER

A sense of self is explored through pretend activities in which children try on other identities. Dressing up as a cook one day and a bus driver the next allows children to try on different personalities and behaviors. These imaginative experiences help to form a child's identity and should be encouraged.

The growing sense of self in preschoolers also includes the awareness of gender. Younger preschoolers understand that they are either a boy or a girl, but they may still think it possible that their sex will change someday. By the age of 5, they realize that gender is a lifelong trait. As their identity with one sex develops, preschoolers become aware that specific gender differences exist—they see very clearly that a boy's ways of dressing, playing, and behaving are often quite different from a girl's. This is also the time when gender stereotypes are introduced. Boys are frequently scolded for crying, while girls are soothed and comforted. Girls are scolded for running around wildly, while boys are praised for their physical adventures. Research shows that boys are the recipients of harsh discipline–spanking, hitting, verbal abuse–more often than girls. Girls are encouraged to cuddle with their stuffed animals, while boys are given blocks and trucks. Preschoolers are quick to pick up what adults consider right and wrong for their sex.

You can give your child a more well-rounded view of gender roles by making an effort to balance the scales. There's no need to take action figures away from your son or dolls away from your daughter; just make sure both kinds of toys are available to both sexes. You don't have to squash your daughter's sympathetic and nurturing qualities as long as her assertiveness and athletic abilities are also encouraged. It's fine to encourage your son's love of physical adventure, but it's also important to teach him about the feelings of others and how to express anger with words rather than fists. By giving your children the freedom to be both tough and tender, regardless of their sex, you give them a sense of identity that is free from the constrictions of stereotypes.

Parenting to Help Children Develop a Sense of Self

- Encourage your child to describe himself to express his self-image.
- Ask your child to describe how someone else might describe her.

JUST A PHASE?

Warning signs that your child may have gender identity confusion are the following:

- **Your child does not know his or her own sex by age 3.**
- **Your child, 3 years or older, consistently says that he or she prefers to be the opposite sex.**
- **Your child consistently speaks ill of or denies his or her own sexual anatomy.**
- **Your child insists that he or she will develop the sexual anatomy of the opposite sex.**

If one or more of these warning signs are present, you should seek professional consultation to help you and your child deal with the issue of sexual identity.

- Encourage your child's pretend dress-up play.
- Make sure your child has access to both "boy" and "girl" toys.
- Give your child the freedom to be both tough and tender, regardless of the child's sex.
- Encourage positive self-image in your child by making him feel capable, special, and worthy.
- Help your child understand that she doesn't have to be perfect to feel good about herself.

Avoid

- Scolding boys for crying.
- Scolding girls for running around when the boys are allowed to.
- Overdoing false praise that gives your child an unrealistic self-picture.
- Telling your child she is the best at everything.
- Making excuses for or denying the fact that other children may do some things better than your child.

REMEMBER

As preschoolers observe and experience the world, their sense of who they are begins to broaden.

Autonomy

Preschoolers are getting very good at doing many things independently. In this age group, children are generally fully toilet trained. They can dress and undress themselves, and they can speak in full sentences. Eventually they learn to cut with safety scissors and even to write their own names. Each activity that a child attacks and conquers feeds that child's growing sense of autonomy—the core of self-confidence.

Of course all parents want their children eventually to be self-sufficient, but it can be very difficult to let it happen now when children's physical skills and their judgment of consequences are not yet up to par with their intentions. They want to tie their shoes, but it takes forever. They want to pour their juice, but they'll probably spill it. They want to ride a bicycle without training wheels, but they may fall. They want to try lots of things that you can do for them faster, better, and safer yourself.

Children who aim high and want to try it all often find their path to autonomy blocked by their parents. They may be punished, discouraged, or frightened away from exploring and conquering their world. Sometimes this is necessary (a 5-year-old should not be allowed to cross the highway alone to visit a friend), but other times it is not. When children are made to feel anxious about their need for autonomy, they generally learn to deny, minimize, or disguise this need, prolonging their dependence on their parents (sometimes far beyond childhood).

There are three guidelines that can help you build your preschooler's sense of autonomy:

Choose your battles wisely. If your day is full of arguments and battles with your preschooler, it may be because you are trying to control every aspect of her life and are giving her no room to think for herself. You are not choosing your battles wisely if you spend your day saying no: "No, you can't wear that shirt with those pants." "No, you can't put peanut butter on lettuce." "No, you can't try that puzzle; it's too hard for you." The next time you begin to say no, stop and think if anyone will get hurt if you say yes. If everyone stays safe, teach yourself to overlook a lot of little things. Reserve your *no*s for things that affect the safety or well-being of your child or others.

Increase your level of tolerance. How much of a mess can you tolerate? How long are you willing to wait to get a simple task completed? Can you bear to have your preschooler sweep the floor even though he doesn't do it as well as you do it? The answers to these questions give you an idea of where your tolerance level rests. Becoming self-sufficient requires a lot of time and patience–on everyone's part. Try to increase your tolerance level by allowing for

SCIENCE TO TAKE HOME

An experiment with more than 100 children of nursery school age points to a link between parental hostility and child dependency (Marshall, 1961). The parents of these children filled out a questionnaire designed to measure their hostility. Results showed that parents who scored high in hostility toward, or rejection of, their children had offspring who were very dependent on other adults, as indicated by observation. The children exhibited their dependence by frequently asking their teachers for help and seeking their approval.

less than perfection when your child tries to do something by himself. Accept the mess as part of the learning process when your child wants to help you make dinner. Build extra time into your schedule so you can give your child the 15 minutes he needs to make his own lunch, or tie his own shoes, or put on his own coat. We all know you can do things better and faster, but your child needs to know he can do it himself, no matter how long it takes or how messy or incomplete the end result is.

Watch what you say. When children try to do things for themselves they usually do it wrong at first. When they fail or fall short of their goal, think before you speak. What would you say if your child spilled the juice trying to pour it into her cup? You could say, "Next time ask me; I'll do it for you." Or you might say, "Look at the mess you made!" Or, you might say, "You know you can't do that without spilling it!" These are all common responses, but each one tells the child that she is incapable of doing things herself. To build self-confidence and encourage autonomy, you might say, "You almost did that just right. Try it again, but let's pull your chair over to the sink and put your cup in the sink so that if it spills, you can easily clean it up." Or you might say, "Here, let me put the juice in a smaller container so you can better pour it without spilling." Spilled juice is no big deal; your child's fragile sense of autonomy is—so remember to think before you speak.

CONSIDER

Some timid children need their parents' encouragement to explore the world and gain a sense of accomplishment. If your preschooler clings to your leg, don't encourage this dependency. Instead, gently suggest that your child move away and try new things (with your assurance that you will be near by if the child needs you).

Parenting to Nurture Autonomy

- Give your preschooler lots of opportunities to find out how the world and the people in it work.
- Reserve the word *no* for things that negatively affect the safety or well-being of your child or others.
- Give your child time and space to do things for himself.
- When your child makes a mistake, think before you speak. Try to say something encouraging so she will not be afraid to try again.

Avoid

- Punishing, discouraging, or frightening your child when he tries to explore his world in a safe environment.

- Trying to control your child so she doesn't have an opportunity to think for herself.
- Denying your child an experience because you're afraid he'll make a mess or do it incorrectly.
- Scolding your child for trying to do things herself—even when they don't work out just right.

REMEMBER

Each activity that your child learns to master independently feeds his or her growing sense of autonomy—the core of self-confidence.

Responsibility

Preschoolers are not exactly what one would call *responsible*. They cannot always remember to put their dirty clothes in the hamper; they can't be counted on to clean up their toys; they don't brush their teeth without constant reminders. They simply don't see why they should put obligations before fun. This natural aversion to acting responsibly makes it tough to get preschoolers to help out, clean up after themselves, and show care and concern for others. And who has time to show them how? In our hectic world, it's easy to deny young children the opportunity to gain a sense of responsibility because we're just too tired and too busy.

"I thought it would be a good idea if Jason set the table every night," says Jason's mom, Lynda. "But he's so slow, and he usually drops the napkins and forks, so I don't even ask him to do it anymore." Lynda's original plan was a good one. Setting the table is a good chore for preschoolers because it is something they are capable of doing. It contributes to the entire family, and it reinforces the concept of right and left. But because he couldn't immediately do it fast enough and perfect enough, Jason wasn't allowed to persist, learn, and contribute. Don't let your preschooler's resistance or lack of skills deprive him of the opportunity to act responsibly. Eventually, having your child do chores around the house will make things easier for you, but in the beginning, it takes time and patience to help your child learn how to be a responsible person.

In this age group, chores are valuable learning tools. Not only do they teach responsibility, they also boost a child's sense of social significance and family contribution—they make a child feel useful and competent, which builds self-reliance and self-esteem. How great a 4-year-old feels when he helps his tired mother fold the laundry (without realizing, of course, that this tired mother will probably have to

AGE DIFFERENCES

Make sure the chore you assign your preschooler is age-appropriate. If the task is beyond your child's capability level, the result will be messy and frustrating—weakening rather than strengthening self-esteem. A 3-year-old can sort the laundry; a 6-year-old can learn to fold it. A 3-year-old can wipe the table with a sponge; a 6-year-old can clear the dishes off the table and then wipe it clean. A 3-year-old can put dirty silverware in the dishwasher; a 6-year-old can sort and put away clean silverware.

refold every piece when the child leaves the room). What a wonderful feeling of accomplishment a 5-year-old feels when she helps wash the family car. How proud a 3-year-old feels when he makes the family a salad by putting the leaves of lettuce in the salad bowl. With this much to gain, it's obviously worth the time it takes to get your child into the habit of helping around the house.

Children this age can also begin to take responsibility for dressing themselves. Let them struggle with zippers, buttons, and bows. Their fine motor skills are maturing, making this an optimal time to take on these tasks. Shoelace tying can be especially problematic, but don't despair and resort to Velcro if your child doesn't catch on quickly; this won't help her master the skill. Just keep giving the child opportunities to practice. You might get an interactive book that has real tying shoelaces inside, such as *Red Lace, Yellow Lace: Learn to Tie Your Shoe* by Mike Casey (Barron's Educational Series, 1996).

When you assign chores, follow these four guidelines:

SCIENCE TO TAKE HOME

Chores can encourage compassion and sensitivity. According to a University of Toronto study, kids who have routine chores are more likely to be considerate of others than those who don't. They express thoughtfulness in spontaneous acts, like comforting someone who's sad or lending a hand without being asked (Grusec, Goodnow, & Cohen 1997).

Work alongside your child at first. Show him how the job is done. Take turns doing it correctly. First you sort some socks from the laundry basket, then let your child give it a try. First you put some food in the dog's bowl, then let your child finish the job. Remember to be patient and tolerant. Even with lots of practice, your child cannot do the job as well as you can. Lower your standards of perfection a bit to allow your child the chance to contribute. (If you need to redo a job, wait until your child is out of the room.)

Praise the effort. Every time your child does a chore without complaining, be sure to voice your appreciation. She'll quickly find that she likes getting positive attention for helping you and will become more willing to do it again and again.

Build the habit. Chores are most willingly done when they are a routine part of each day's schedule. If it's your child's job to put the toys away at the end of the day, set aside a specific time for this task. It won't take long before your child begins to clean up without being reminded as soon as you announce, "It's seven o'clock!" If it's your child's job to bring her plate to the kitchen sink after dinner *every* night, eventually she won't need reminders. If you want your child to make his bed each morning, make sure you enforce the rule *every* morning. Soon this won't be a point of contention; it will be just another part of the day.

Set up a reward system if your child persistently resists doing chores. Put a star on a sticker chart every time your child completes an assigned task on time, and offer a reward when there are five stars on the chart. Ask your child to choose a reward for doing the chores (offer reasonable options such as an ice-cream cone or a video rental rather than a new bike or a trip to the amusement park).

Give your child a job that will build a sense of responsibility even if you can do the task far better and faster yourself. At this young age it's not the end result that is most important; it's the fact that chores help children in their struggle to feel valuable, helpful, and competent.

Parenting to Teach Responsibility

- Remember that preschoolers need your help to learn how to be responsible.
- Accept that it takes time and patience to help your child learn how to be a responsible person.
- Assign chores that are age-appropriate.
- Show your child how the job is done before expecting her to do it correctly.
- Praise your child's efforts and accomplishments.
- Schedule daily time for chores so they soon become a habit.
- Offer rewards to overcome initial resistance or difficulty remembering a chore.

CONSIDER

Chores should not be assigned as punishment. This sends the message that contributing to the family is undesirable work and chores are the consequence of unacceptable behavior. Children cannot develop a positive attitude about helping others if they learn to associate the act with punishment.

Avoid

- Doing chores yourself because it's easier than getting your child to do them.
- Letting your preschooler's resistance or lack of skills let him off the hook.
- Expecting perfection. Leave lots of room for mistakes and sloppy results.
- Being inconsistent in your expectations. If you want your child to make her bed, make sure it's done every morning.
- Using chores as a punishment.

REMEMBER

Giving your preschooler a daily chore will build his or her sense of responsibility (even if you can do the task far better and faster yourself).

Character Formation

Preschoolers are now able to see the world from another person's viewpoint, and this makes all the difference in the way they understand the concepts of right and wrong, good and bad, and polite and rude. Children this age are ready to use their growing sense of empathy to act in ways that don't hurt or insult other people. They can now understand why they should be kind, honest, obedient, and polite, but they aren't yet quite ready to always remember the rules that govern morals, discipline, and manners. They need lots of reminders–and parents need lots of patience.

Values and Morals

It is during the preschool years that you will first see signs of a developing conscience. Children now recognize that there is a set of standards of acceptable behavior, they can now act in accordance with those standards, and they feel guilty if they violate them. But like other aspects of a preschooler's thinking, your child looks at these standards in a very concrete way. In this stage, called *moral realism,* the "right" way is sacred, inflexible, and untouchable. Rules are made by a superior authority and cannot be bent or broken. This kind of reasoning makes it difficult for young children to evaluate moral dilemmas that require the ability to distinguish between intent and behavior. For example, they see no difference between breaking a dish by accident and breaking it on purpose–the end result is the same. In fact, preschoolers are sure that the person who breaks five dishes by accidentally dropping them is much naughtier than the person who intentionally breaks one dish by throwing it on the floor. The rightness or wrongness of an act resides in the act itself, not in the intention behind it.

This developing concept of what's right and what's wrong and the increasing ability to see another person's viewpoint leads preschoolers

AGE DIFFERENCES

At age 3, children will play a game each in their own way, following their own set of rules. By age 5, however, the rules are absolute and must be followed the same way by all, with no exceptions. When asked if children in a different country play the game with the exact same rules, the 5-year-old will insist that they must.

to prosocial behaviors based on feelings of empathy. They will often surprise you with acts of altruism such as offers of comfort, sympathy, assistance, sharing, cooperation, and protection—all offered with unselfish concern for the welfare of others. This is an important step away from the egocentric view of life they have lived with up to this point.

The concepts of right and wrong and the value of unselfish concern for others are slowly learned throughout this age period. Preschoolers continually add to their understanding of values and morals in four ways:

- *Experiential learning.* When children are rewarded for an act they learn that it is right and good. When they are scolded or punished, they learn that it is bad.
- *Observational learning.* Children learn by watching the experiences of others. If your child observes another child being scolded for hitting a playmate, she will vicariously learn that this behavior is unacceptable. Likewise, the more often she sees others being praised for helping a playmate, the more she is likely to want to be helpful.
- *Imitation.* Children will often imitate a role model they identify with—usually parents and teachers. This identification teaches young children many lessons, both intentional and unintentional. A parent's words about the value of honesty, for example, have no sticking power if the child hears Dad lie about the child's age in order to purchase a reduced-rate admission ticket. On the other hand, lessons about helping others mean very little until the child sees his parents gathering clothes for the poor or volunteering their time to a local charity.
- *Role-playing.* This favored childhood game is often used to help children learn about right and wrong behaviors. Pretending games allow children to act out roles and learn how to see things from another's point of view. Sometimes children are presented with a moral dilemma and asked to play the roles of different characters and to try to figure out what the characters should do to solve their problem. A teacher or parent might say, for example, "Katie has fallen down and scraped her knee. What should her friend Jon-

CONSIDER

Children learn about right and wrong by imitating their parents. How confusing it must be when a parent slaps a child's hands for hitting another child. "This will teach you to never hit anyone," the parent will say while hitting the child. It is very important that parents' actions not contradict their words.

athan do?" Acting out the parts of Katie and Jonathan, children can think about how they might offer comfort, get a Band-Aid, or call for help. Researchers have found that role-playing increases the willingness of children to help others and that the effect can last for as long as a week.

SCIENCE TO TAKE HOME

Children's prosocial behaviors are affected by what they watch on television. When groups of preschoolers were exposed to violent cartoons, *Mr. Rogers' Neighborhood,* or neutral films, the children exposed to the prosocial programs displayed more prosocial behavior than children in the other groups (Friedrich & Stein, 1975).

During this learning stage, preschoolers are not yet quite ready to let their conscience be their guide. Although they have learned that it is wrong to cheat at games, take things that don't belong to them, lie to their parents, and hit their friends, they still will do these things more often than not. It's still just too hard to control impulses. But they do want so much to be good–that's why they'll lie when they've broken a rule. When your preschooler's actions appear to contradict what she's learned about values and morals, be patient and gentle. A broken rule gives you a good opportunity to state the rule again and explain the reasoning behind it. This is the perfect time to state, "Kicking is not allowed; it hurts your friend." Then appeal to your child's sense of fairness and compassion: "Kyle looks sad because you hurt him." This will help your child understand how one's actions affect other people, and that's what a moral conscience is all about.

Parenting to Teach Values and Morals

- Understand that to your child's way of thinking, the rightness or wrongness of an act resides in the act itself, not in the intention behind it.
- Praise your child when he shows unselfish concern for the welfare of others.
- Reward your child when she follows the rules. Scold her when she breaks the rules.
- Be aware that your child learns a great deal about what's right and wrong by watching you.
- Role-play moral situations with your child to give him practice in choosing the right solution.
- When your child breaks a rule, use the opportunity to restate the rule and the reason behind it.

REMEMBER

The developing concept of what's right and what's wrong and the increasing ability to see another person's viewpoint leads preschoolers to prosocial behaviors based on feelings of empathy.

Avoid

- Expecting your child to understand that rules can be bent to fit the circumstance.
- Letting your actions contradicts your words.
- Lying, cheating, hitting, or stealing if you don't want your child to do the same.
- Expecting preschoolers to control their impulses when they know something is wrong but want to do it anyway.

Self-Control and Discipline

You'll find that your preschooler is now more willing to be obedient and is more anxious to please than was your toddler. This is a welcome break from the previous years that were often filled with temper tantrums and incessant refusals to do anything you asked. But because your child is now a bit easier to handle doesn't mean he needs less discipline. Remember, *discipline* is another word for *teaching,* which is an ongoing process throughout childhood and adolescence.

SCIENCE TO TAKE HOME

Three-year-olds are more likely than toddlers to do what their parents tell them and less likely to break rules when their parents are not looking, which may be a sign of their developing sense of morality (Emde & Buchsbaum, 1990).

Diana Baumrind (1967, 1968, 1971) has extensively investigated three types of parenting styles and their effects on children. She has called these styles *authoritarian, permissive,* and *authoritative.* Her findings may help you adapt your style to the one that is best for your child.

Authoritarian Style

The style. Authoritarian parents expect rigid, unquestioning obedience. They attempt to shape their children's behavior according to precise and absolute standards of conduct. Rules and regulations are set in concrete, and yelling, hitting, and the threat of force are often used to assure compliance. This parenting style does not allow for discussion or explanation. The child's role is to respect authority and to obey without question.

The results. A number of studies have found that children raised in authoritarian households display a lesser degree of internal moral control (or conscience) than do children exposed to other child-rearing patterns. Authoritarian parents tend to produce withdrawn, fearful children who exhibit little or no independence and are moody, unassertive, and irritable. This rigid form of discipline teaches children that they are incapable of asserting any control over their own lives. If a child in an authoritarian household wants a snack before dinner, the issue is clear-cut: no snack before dinner. No discussion. That's the rule.

Permissive Style

The style. Permissive parents are the extreme opposite of authoritarian parents. They are so intent on showing their children unconditional love that they rarely set limits or say no. These parents value a child's freedom, individuality, and verbal expressiveness. They attempt to control or shape their child's behavior primarily by reasoning and infrequently punish behavioral problems. Their children have much freedom, but little guidance.

The results. Children raised in permissive households tend to be impulsive, immature, and more aggressive than other children. The lack of structure in their homes not only encourages demanding, inconsiderate behavior, but also fails to teach self-control. If a child in a permissive household wants a snack before dinner, the child takes one. There is no rule against it and no need to even ask permission.

Authoritative Style

The style. Authoritative parents stand in the middle between authoritarian and permissive parents. They exercise control over their children's behavior, but they do it with some degree of flexibility. They are willing to reason with their children, to explain rules, and

---

CONSIDER

Permissive parents are not the same as indifferent parents. Permissive parents love their children and want the best for them. Indifferent parents have little interest in their children's activities and are most concerned with their own comfort and convenience. Children raised by indifferent parents who fail to discipline because of the time and trouble involved have the most behavioral problems of all. They tend to lack self-confidence, have lowered self-esteem and lowered achievement motivation, and are impulsive, moody, and disobedient.

AGE DIFFERENCES

The authoritative method of discipline achieves the best results regardless of the child's age. Children of all ages respond best to discipline from parents who are firm yet warm and caring.

to allow for appropriate degrees of independence. They encourage verbal give-and-take, but their children know that on important issues, the parents are the boss. Authoritative parents set firm limits and expect much, but at the same time they are warm, supportive, and respectful of their children's needs and interests.

The results. Children raised in authoritative households have been found to be the most well adjusted. They are the most self-reliant, self-controlled, and socially competent. They are also the most independent and achievement-oriented. These children are most likely to do very well in school and to avoid adolescent behavior problems such as drug and alcohol abuse. If a child in an authoritative household wants a snack before dinner, the parents will consider if there is a legitimate reason why the child might be too hungry to wait for dinner. If so, the child might be told that a piece of chocolate cake is out of the question, but a piece of fruit or some raw vegetables would be all right.

JUST A PHASE?

If most of the time your preschooler fails to comply with your specific commands, it is likely that your child has a noncompliance problem. This should not be allowed to continue past the preschool stage. The child needs to learn to follow adult directions most of the time.

The goal of discipline is to give children the skills, knowledge, and values they need to participate successfully in society. The authoritative style of parenting has been found to be most helpful in reaching this goal. If you can be both demanding and yet responsive and warm, you will teach your child how to be confident and assertive, yet respectful and obedient. This is not always easy to do, but well worth the effort.

Parenting to Teach Self-Control

- Examine your parenting style to determine if it is authoritarian, permissive, or authoritative.
- Strive to use an authoritative parenting style that offers firm limits as well as warmth and understanding.
- Set limits to control your child's behavior, but adjust them to fit the child's changing needs and abilities.

Avoid

- Using an authoritarian parenting style that is rigid and demanding, allowing for little discussion or explanation.

- Using a permissive parenting style that avoids firm limits and offers little guidance.
- Being an indifferent parent who fails to discipline because it requires too much time and effort.

REMEMBER

Of the three parenting styles (authoritarian, permissive, and authoritative), the authoritative style is most likely to give children the guidance they need to be well adjusted, self-controlled, and socially responsible.

Manners

Manners aren't only about using the right fork; they're about being kind and making people feel at ease–giving compliments, saying thank you, holding doors, and waiting a turn to speak. These things require tiny sacrifices for the sake of another person–something that preschoolers are ready to do (sometimes). Your child's newfound sense of empathy allows him to begin thinking about how other people feel, but it doesn't yet come naturally. He is still very curious, impulsive, and totally lacking in diplomacy, so he'll need your help and constant reminders to become well mannered.

When preschoolers are rude, it is rarely intentional. It's just that they are too impulsive to think before they speak or act. This is why 4-year-old Juanita loudly announced, "This tastes yucky!" after tasting her aunt's special holiday dinner. This is why 5-year-old Kendra yelled out as she pointed to the man in front of her on the supermarket line, "Look, that man has no hair!" This is why 3-year-old Martin snuggled on his grandmother's lap and calmly asked, "Why are you so fat?" These children shouldn't be punished for their rudeness, but they are now old enough to be instructed about good manners.

Because of their improved language skills you can talk to children this age about manners. The lessons will have the greatest impact if you talk about a specific situation–in private. Before you go to a relative's house for dinner, for example, explain to your child that she may not like the food that's offered. Then help her see that it would hurt the relative's feelings if she said something like "Yuck. I don't want this. It tastes bad." Instead, teach her to say nothing and to politely say "No thank you" if she is offered more.

If your child makes a rude comment that you can't intercept, quickly change the subject. If you make a scene by scolding him, saying, "Jimmy! That's not nice. Say you're sorry right now," you'll embarrass and shame your child for something he didn't mean to do, and that's bad manners. Instead, wait until the two of you are alone and explain why this kind of comment hurts people's feelings and that you don't want him to say it again. This lesson teaches your child to respect other people's feelings, which is what manners is really all about.

The best way to teach manners is through your own example. This is another reason why it's never a good idea to scold your child publicly for having bad manners. By refraining from humiliating your child in front of others, you teach her that feelings matter. Being rude to your child because she was rude to someone else is like hitting a child to teach her not to hit anyone–it sends a confusing message. It's important to be aware of how you treat others. Speak kindly to your spouse. Speak politely to the grocer. Hold your temper if another driver cuts you off. If you want your child to be polite and civilized, she needs to see how it works.

SCIENCE TO TAKE HOME

In a social development study of 3- to 5-year-olds, researchers observed the level of politeness the children used when faced with a conflict. They found that when the other party gave reasons for refusing a child's request, the children showed greater levels of politeness in their response. This politeness level dropped when no reason was given for a refusal (Leonard, 1993).

Role-playing is a direct and fun way to teach young children how to behave politely. Let's say you're bringing your child with you on a quick trip to your place of business. If you don't want to be embarrassed, it's a good idea to take a few minutes to act out how you want your child to behave. Practice saying hello and goodbye. Work on standing quietly and still. It's sometimes fun to switch roles so you can act out the behavior of a child who is unmannerly. Whine, jump around, and interrupt to let your child (who is pretending to be you) see why that kind of behavior is rude.

You can role-play many situations to teach good manners. Your child is now old enough to use the phone and therefore old enough to use good phone manners. Make a game out of answering the phone politely; teach your child to say something like "Hello. Who is calling please?" Practice calling friends with a friendly "Hello, this is David. May I speak to Mary, please?" You can also role-play to teach table manners. Although preschoolers are old enough to learn basic rules such as elbows off the table, napkins on lap, and no chewing with mouth wide open, they are not yet ready to always remember the rules. Your child needs many opportunities to practice these skills before he can comfortably use them in real-life situations.

CONSIDER

If your previously polite child suddenly begins ordering you around and refuses to say please, don't lose your cool. Saying "Get me juice!" may be a sign that there's a power struggle going on. If you insist that you won't get the juice until your child says "Please," and you stand firm and stay under emotional control, you will probably get compliance.

You will need to remind your children about their manners very often. They're old enough to learn them, but not yet old enough to remember them immediately (especially when they're excited because you have company or it's a holiday and you'd most especially like them to be polite). Don't give up on the lessons you introduced to your children as toddlers: Continue to remind them to say "Please," "Thank you," and "Excuse me." When they forget and appear rude, don't return the rudeness with rudeness of your own; simply remind them of your expectations and add a positive note that you're sure they'll remember next time.

CONSIDER

By age 5, children are able to consider another person's point of view. Before your child has a friend over for a play date, talk about ways she can make her friend feel at home. For instance, your child might offer her friend a few choices of things to do and ask her if she'd like something to eat or drink.

Parenting to Teach Good Manners

- Remember that when preschoolers are rude, it is rarely intentional.
- Use specific situations such as dinner time to talk about manners.
- Use your own example of good manners to teach your child how to be polite.
- Practice mannerly behavior with your child by role-playing situations such as talking on the telephone.

Avoid

- Punishing your children for rude behavior.
- Publicly shaming your child for bad manners.
- Speaking rudely to others.
- Expecting preschoolers to always remember the good manners you teach them.
- Giving up on your reminders to politely say "Please," "Thank you," and "Excuse me."

REMEMBER

Your child's newfound sense of empathy allows him to begin thinking about how other people feel, but it doesn't yet come naturally. He is still very curious, impulsive, and totally lacking in diplomacy, so he'll need your help and constant reminders to become well mannered.

6 to 9 Years

STAGE 4

Dear Diary,

Can it really be that Christopher is 9 years old? He's turned into such a little man overnight. Suddenly I can't hold his hand when we cross the street, and heaven forbid I should kiss him goodbye in front of his friends! Thank goodness he's not too old to be tucked in at night. At bedtime he's willing to let down his "big boy" guard and cuddle up for a goodnight kiss and a hug. During the day I can usually get his attention by challenging him with a riddle; he especially likes jokes that play on words. It makes me feel so good to see him laugh out loud and show his sense of humor. Of course, there are other times when things don't go his way and he shows another side of himself. Christopher has quite a temper that he's slowly learning to control. I've noticed that he is especially apt to get angry when he feels embarrassed. It's like he doesn't want anyone to know that he is capable of making a mistake.

I'm impressed by how well Christopher has learned to read and write. Three years ago, he had just learned to write his name; now he's reading whole books and writing book reports. I'm tempted to buy him some workbooks that would help him practice the skills he's learning in school, but his teacher says that's not such a good idea. She says it would be more helpful if I used the time to build up his vocabulary just by having a conversation with him or if I gave him background experiences by taking trips to interesting places. She says that reading aloud to him is still a good way to help improve his reading skills. All this sounds a lot better to me than making him complete a drill workbook.

The activities that support Christopher's reading and writing skills also give us some valuable time together. I try to set aside an hour every Saturday morning just for us. Sometimes we go shopping, or we go to the park, or we bake something at home, or we just play a board game and hang out. Whatever it is, it's a special time for us. Without this scheduled time I think I'd feel left out; Christopher is always rushing off to do something with his good friend, Pete. Although I confess that I sometimes feel a little jealous of the time those two spend together, I have to admit that they are quite a team. They take care of each other and are most often very kind and considerate of each other's feelings. They're both learning how to be a good friend. I'm hoping that this kind of relationship will help both of them resist peer pressure and the need to follow the crowd.

Now that Christopher has a special group of friends, he often wants to do things that I'm not so sure he's ready to do. Last week he told me that "the guys" were all going to meet at the movies and nobody's mom or dad was going to go in with them. Maybe I worry too much, but it's hard to know where the line is between being a good parent and being overprotective. I let him go, but I was at the door to pick him up the minute the film was over. With every inch of new ground my son covers I feel like pulling him back to the safety of our home, but of course I don't. There's a rational side of me that realizes he can't grow into a confident, responsible grown-up if I never give him opportunities to be independent. The upside of this is that I've also realized that if he is old enough to be trusted to be responsible, he's old enough to be given responsibilities around the house also. Christopher's chore list is not very demanding, but it's very helpful to me when he chips in and cleans his own room, sweeps the floor after dinner, and takes out the garbage.

Usually, Christopher does what he's told without too much of a problem, but sometimes he acts up, almost like he's testing me to see if I really mean it. I read somewhere that kids will learn best from discipline tactics that offer both punishments for breaking the family rules and rewards for keeping them. This system works well in our house. When I'm there to watch him, I know Christopher knows what's right and wrong. My hope is that he will be able to do the right thing even when I'm not there to influence him. I think he's on the right track–the other night at the shopping mall I saw him hold the door open for an elderly couple. I think my little man is going to grow into a wonderful human being

Emotional Health

The emotional life of school-age children is full of ups and downs, laughs and tears. The challenge of parenting through these years is to understand and respect the changes these children are experiencing and help them over the rough spots and guide them around the pitfalls. They still want lots of love and affection, but they don't want anyone to see you give it. (Try kissing your third grader in front of his friends!) They need someone to help them recognize angry feelings and deal with them before they get out of control. And they need encouragement to get over the fear of peer ridicule that may keep them from taking risks and exploring their capabilities. Parents who can do these things for their children help them grow up feeling secure and confident.

Love and Affection

In the elementary school years, your children still need lots of love and affection–but they sure don't want other people to know it (as you'll find out if you try to hold your child's hand on the way to school where other children might see). Children ages 6 to 9 continue to struggle for independence at the same time that they need much emotional support. Your job during this stage is to let your children know that they are always loved and to convey that message in ways that are comfortable for them to accept.

Unconditional love is the most valuable gift you can give your child. It is love that does not have to be earned–not by school achievement, not by good behavior, and not by athletic accomplishments. It is given freely with no strings attached. This love seems like the most natural kind for parents to give, but in our success-driven society the gift of love often gets turned into a reward for accomplishment. It's natural to give our children a big kiss when they bring home a good report card, and a hearty hug when they score the winning goal–but if these are the

RESEARCH

Just at the time when children are learning about loving relationships by watching their parents, many parents separate and divorce. The way children respond to divorce is influenced by the nature of the parent-child relationship. Long-term involvement and emotional support from a parent (or better still, from both parents) help the child make a successful adjustment. In fact, the nature of the ongoing parent-child interaction is much more important than whether both parents are present in the home (Rutter & Garmezy, 1983).

CONSIDER

Avoid statements that indicate to your children that they are loved only for what they do. Avoid comments like "I love you because you're such a good boy," or "Who could love such a naughty child?" Don't make your children feel there is a connection between their behavior and your love.

only kinds of circumstances in which they get signs of affection, we may be sending the wrong message. Your children need to know that you love them for who they are, not for what they do. More than anything else, this is what makes children feel secure and good about themselves and builds self-esteem and strong mental health.

Sometimes giving unconditional love takes a conscious, concerted effort. To see for yourself how easy it is to withhold "no-occasion" love and affection, look back at the day as your children head for bed. You might find that much of the energy focused on your kids has been about getting things done–getting them to school, preparing their dinner, and transporting them to activities. It's likely that there just wasn't a moment at all that said to your child, "I love you." And because your children are now so involved with school and friends and other activities, they're less likely to jump into your lap asking for that reassuring hug.

SEX DIFFERENCES

Children ages 6 to 9 are increasingly able to extend affectionate feelings outward, away from the immediate family and toward teachers and friends. Girls tend to form more openly affectionate attachments to same-sex friends than boys do. Boys tend to express affection indirectly and nonverbally, with a friendly punch, for example, instead of a hug.

Make time every day for one-on-one quality time to let your kids know they're very special to you. This might be while driving in the car or while fixing dinner together. It might be at bedtime when you spend just a few quiet minutes together. Kids feel your affection most when they have you all to themselves–even if only for 15 minutes.

You can also send your children messages of unconditional love when they least expect it. When you walk by your child, occasionally bend down and kiss his head. Send a little note to school in her lunch bag that says, "I hope you're having a great day!" Bring home a bunch of flowers for your daughter or a treat for your son–for no special reason. Schedule dates for a fun time out of the home with each

AGE DIFFERENCES

Around age 6, children may "fall in love" with their teacher or with a playmate of the opposite sex. Although it's only puppy love, these early relationships express children's genuine feelings. As they approach the age of 8 or 9, boys may declare "Love is gross," and girls may insist "Boys are yucky." This is their way of distancing themselves from emotions that make them feel vulnerable and uncomfortable.

child. There are lots of ways to say "I love you"–try to find one each and every day.

Parenting to Nurture Love and Affection

- Give love freely with no strings attached.
- Love your children for who they are, not for what they do.
- Make a habit of giving your child a sign of your love every day.
- Try to find some one-on-one time each day with your child.
- Respect your child's crush on a teacher or playmate.

Avoid

- Giving your children signs of love and affection only when they have achieved some accomplishment.
- Making comments that tie your love to a particular behavior (i.e., "I love you because you're so smart").
- Letting the day go by without giving your child a clear message of love and affection.
- Ridiculing your child's experiences with puppy love.

REMEMBER

Unconditional love is the most valuable gift you can give your child.

Joy and Anger

A source of joy to children ages 6 to 9 is a good joke. Their verbal skills are now so well developed that they can manipulate word meanings for a good sidesplitting laugh. Jokes like "What has an ear but can't hear? Corn!" are especially uproarious when they test the intelligence of adults; this lets these kids feel mentally superior, if only for a moment. Now is a good time to buy your kids a book of riddles and use daily jokes to challenge their mental growth. This sort of playful think-

SCIENCE TO TAKE HOME

Researchers Norman Prentice and Robert Fathom (1972) have found that there is a positive relationship between cognitive maturity and comprehension of joking riddles.

ing teaches children to think flexibly and creatively while they're having a great time.

Humor can also be used at this stage to soften the edges on those occasional bad moods before they have a chance to turn into angry outbursts. For example, 8-year-old Lori was in a bad mood because her father told her to sweep the floor. Her incessant whining drove her dad, Wayne, to shout, "That's it! This is now an official 'Be-Sad' Chore." Sitting down with an exaggerated frown he continued, "Neither of us can smile until you're done. No laughing, no giggling, no chuckling, no snickering. No fun allowed at all!" As Wayne continued his sad routine, Lori began to laugh. "Don't you dare," Wayne reminded her. "No smiles allowed until you're finished." The more Wayne frowned, the sillier he looked to Lori who was soon giggling and jumping around trying to coax Wayne into laughter.

This little exercise in silliness is helping Lori develop a sense of humor–which is more than just the ability to tell jokes. It's an attitude that can diffuse tension, cushion life's blows, put problems into perspective, and help children handle their feelings of anger.

Anger is the emotion that elementary school children still struggle to control. They are now better able to put their feelings into words and will assertively tell a playmate who takes a toy, "Hey, give me that back!" But they are still prone to give in to the physical impulse to hit or push when words don't work right away. The ability to keep angry

GENDER DIFFERENCES

Carol Gilligan, a psychologist and gender issues expert at Harvard University, says that girls are likelier than boys to have trouble expressing anger. Personal relationships are so important to girls that they fear doing or saying anything that might cause a rupture. They imagine that if they express what is really on their mind, their mother or friend will get angry and reject them (Tyson, 1999).

On the other hand, if anger is the only emotion that boys are allowed to express, and if they are taught by their parents to shut down their prosocial feelings (empathy and sympathy), then they are more likely to be at risk for violent behavior (especially if they are frequently exposed to violent movies and video games; Kindlon & Thompson, 1999).

feelings in check instead of acting on them is an important developmental step for this age group. Their task is to learn how to constructively express their anger.

You can help your child learn to recognize angry feelings and deal with them before they get out of control. When you see anger rising in your child, identify the feeling: "I see you're feeling very angry." Then offer your child a positive way to get the anger out (rather than deny it or hold it in):

- Instruct your child to count to 10 before he does anything. This will give him time to think before he acts impulsively.
- Help your child practice expressing anger in words. Say to her, "Tell me how you feel right now and why you feel that way." By articulating angry feelings, children learn to be constructively assertive on their own behalf.
- Guide your child to outlets for anger that will make him feel better: Draw the anger on paper, rip up old newspapers, go for a run around the block, or punch a pillow. These kinds of physical activities release anger without hurting others.

It's most important to teach your children how to respond to angry feelings through your own example. This is especially true in the way you react to your child's anger. Try not to get angry because your child is angry. If your child yells a cruel remark at you and you respond by yelling a cruel remark back, you haven't taught the child that hurting other people's feelings is not an appropriate way to verbalize anger. It is important to remain in control of your emotions when your child is howling with anger. Your ability to regulate your own anger will show the child how it's done.

SCIENCE TO TAKE HOME

Parents who are relatively aware and supportive of the expression of emotion have children who are physiologically well regulated and therefore can manage their emotional arousal in social contexts. Children whose fathers tend to respond with negative emotion to their children's displays of negative emotion are less socially skilled—they share less, avoid others more, and are more aggressive (Eisenberg et al., 1999).

Parenting to Help Children Handle Joy and Anger

- Buy your kids a book of riddles and use daily jokes to challenge their mental growth.
- Use humor to soften the edges on those occasional bad moods before they have a chance to turn into angry outbursts.
- Remember that the ability to keep angry feelings in check instead of acting on them is an important developmental step for this age group.
- Help your daughters express their anger so they learn that they will not be rejected for having this emotion.
- When you see anger rising in your child, identify the feeling: "I see you're feeling very angry." Then offer your child a positive way to get the anger out
- Teach your child how to respond to angry feelings through your own example.

Avoid

- Spoiling the fun of your child's jokes by always knowing the punch line.
- Using anger to coax your child out of a bad mood; try humor instead.
- Yelling in anger when your child expresses the emotion of anger.
- Punishing a child who expresses angry feelings.

REMEMBER

The ability to keep feelings in check instead of acting on them is an important developmental step for this age group.

Managing Fear

Just as children get over their preschool fears of imaginary goblins and monsters, they may develop a whole new set of fears rooted in self-consciousness. School-age children are more aware of other people and of themselves as members of a group, and they have a strong need to be accepted by their peers. This makes them fearful of making a mistake, of looking foolish, or of being embarrassed. These fears can be crippling and can keep children from trying new things and exploring the world.

Watch your child for signs of fearful inhibitions. You'll need to respect this fear and at the same time look for ways to help your child conquer it. If, for example, your child doesn't want to try a game of skill at the amusement park (like knocking down the bottles with a ball), don't push him. He may be afraid of failing and feeling embarrassed and that feeling should be respected. But why not give the game a try yourself? If you fail, show your child how you can laugh it off and not let it affect how you feel about yourself.

There are many opportunities to show children that there is no reason to be afraid of making mistakes. If you try a new recipe for dinner and it tastes awful, your reaction to this "failure" will teach your child an important lesson. Don't swear you'll never try anything new again—this teaches children to avoid exploration and risk for fear of disappointment or ridicule. Instead, shrug off this disaster, admitting that anytime you try something new there's always the risk of making a mistake, but that next time you hope the results will be better. Point out that all mistakes are really learning experiences.

Be forgiving, not only of your own mistakes, but of your child's, too. Try not to be critical when your child tries something new and falls short of the mark. This fuels the fear of a challenge. If she spray paints her bike and covers the garage floor with paint as well, take a big breath before you respond. An angry response may say, "That's the last time you'll ever paint anything. Look at the mess you made!" And sure enough, your child will agree that she can't do any projects herself. She'll become afraid to try again. Instead, point out that the next time she wants to paint something, she should make sure that the floor is covered with a drop cloth or newspapers. This turns the mistake into a learning experience and leaves the door open to try again without fear.

Fear of embarrassment and failure is common in school-age children, and with patience and encouragement most will eventually grow out of these inhibitions. However, there are some fears that should no longer be plaguing children of this age. If your child is still clinging to fears from his preschool years that he should have outgrown by now (such as fear of animals, fear of the dark, or fear of clowns), it's time for some action. We recommend a program of systematic desensitization for stubborn fears in school-age children.

Systematic desensitization is a psychological term for slowly and gradually introducing people to the object or circumstance they fear until they feel comfortable and unthreatened. You have heard, for example, that people who are afraid of flying in airplanes can be trained to conquer their fear in small steps that first bring them to the airport, then to the entrance to the plane, then into the plane itself, then to a seat, then to a shuttle out to a runway with an immediate return to the terminal, and then, finally, to actual flight. With this same method of taking small, gradual steps you can help your children overcome many types of fears. Let's take fear of the dark as an example.

To begin the process of desensitization to fear of the dark for a child who will sleep only with a bright light on, we recommend a method that allows you to gradually change the degree of illumination by replacing the wall switch with a rheostat dimmer switch (available in all hardware stores for a few dollars). Once it is installed, use a pencil or crayon to mark the dial with eight degrees, evenly spaced, between the brightest and darkest settings. This will guide your progress as you gradually lower the illumination.

The night you plan to begin the desensitization process, explain to your child that you've thought of a game that will help her get over being afraid to sleep in the dark. Focusing on the fun aspect of this game, tell your child that on the first night she can put the dimmer switch on any setting she'd like. If she chooses the brightest setting, that's fine.

The following night, cheerfully explain that you are now going to lower the light just one notch. Tell her that when she sleeps through the night with this reduced illumination you will reward her in the morning with a prize. (Reveal exactly what the prize will be, and make sure you have it available to give her immediately upon waking.) If your child calls out to wake you in the middle of the night, offer her comfort, but do not offer the prize in the morning. Do, however, give positive assurances that she will do better the next night. If she does sleep through the night, give her the prize as well as praise for the accomplishment.

Leave the light setting at that mark until your child successfully sleeps through three nights without obvious signs of fear. Then move the dimmer dial to the next lower setting, and follow the same routine (praise and reward included) for three more nights. As this program of desensitization moves along, your child will gradually adapt to an ever-darkening room.

Finally, when the brightness level reaches the lowest mark on the dial just before complete darkness, plug a night-light into an electrical outlet in the bedroom and use that in place of the main room light. You

JUST A PHASE?

If a fear persists for more than a year and is no longer age-specific (e.g., an 8-year-old who is still afraid of clowns or the dark), the fear may turn into a phobia, which will prevent the child from participating in normal activities. If your child's fear persists and significantly interferes with his or her daily life, discuss the issue with the child's doctor, who may recommend therapy, which has proven very successful in resolving specific phobias.

may want to progress to a completely darkened room or a darkened one with a night-light in the hall or bathroom. A child who sleeps comfortably through with only a night-light can no longer be considered to be afraid of the dark.

This example gives you an idea how desensitization, with its gradual steps along with praise and reward, can be used to ease a child's fear of almost anything.

Parenting to Help Children Handle Fear

- Watch your child for signs of fearful inhibitions.
- Respect your child's fear of embarrassment, and look for ways to help your child conquer it.
- Show your child that you, too, make mistakes.
- Use mistakes as a learning opportunity.
- Use systematic desensitization methods to help your child get over strong fears of things like the dark, animals, clowns, and so on.

Avoid

- Punishing your child for making a mistake.
- Pushing your child into circumstances that might embarrass her.
- Being critical when your child tries something new and falls short of the mark.
- Suddenly forcing your child to face a fear, such as, shutting him in a darkened room to get over the fear of the dark or throwing her in a swimming pool to overcome the fear of water.

REMEMBER

School-age children are more aware of other people and of themselves as members of a group, and they have a strong need to be accepted by their peers. This makes them fearful of making a mistake, of looking foolish, or of being embarrassed.

Cognitive Development

These are the years when children learn to handle more complex concepts. They can follow directions that have three or four parts. They can now think further into the future, and they can solve abstract problems in their heads. They can form hypotheses about what it might be like to be older, or taller, or live with a different family. Their cognitive growth is especially noticeable in their ability to think about solutions and consequences before they react to a problem; in their play world, where they try on real-life situations; and in their language development, where they are now ready to read and write. In each of these areas, your help and guidance contributes to your child's cognitive development.

Problem Solving

Good problem-solving skills are necessary to negotiate one's way in the world. Children need to learn how to share, take turns, be patient, consider others' needs, and still get what they want and need in the end. Because this is not so easy to do, many children grow up impulsively crying, grabbing, and hitting to solve their problems. Fortunately, it is known that children can learn to diffuse hostility and avoid conflict by thinking before they act, but these problem-solving skills don't come naturally–they need to be taught and practiced.

A particularly good program for teaching children thinking skills that can be used to help resolve or prevent interpersonal problems is the I Can Problem-Solve (ICPS) program created by child psychologist Myrna Shure. In her book *Raising a Thinking Child,* Shure explains that children need to be taught *how* to think, not what to think (Shure, 1994). Shure tells parents that problem-solving skills involve the concepts of alternative solutions and consequential thinking.

Alternative solutions lessons are designed to help children recognize that there is more than one way to solve a problem. Let's say two

CONSIDER

The child who is taught problem-solving skills does not have to be told what to do all the time; the thinking child can consider the needs of others, decide what to do, and evaluate whether the idea is a good one.

children want the same toy at the same time. Their first solution may be to have a tug of war over the toy. Through repeated practice they can learn to stop and think about other ways to get what they want. Instead of intervening and solving the children's problem, you simply ask one of the children, "Can you think of a different way you can get that toy?" The child might say, "I could hit him and then take it." You don't need to evaluate the solution at this point; just acknowledge it and ask for more solutions. The child might continue, "I could trade one of my toys for it," "I could say please," or "I could give him a piece of candy." All these ideas show the child that the first thing that comes to mind when you have a problem is not necessarily the only or the best way to solve that problem.

Consequential thinking skills help children think about what might happen next if a particular solution is carried out. When children are taught to think about consequences before they act, they can better choose actions that do not hurt themselves or others, but are still effective. If a child says he can get the toy the other child has by hitting him, don't jump in to explain why this is not a good solution; the goal is to get children to think for themselves. Ask the child to think about what might happen next. The child might say, "He'll give me the toy." Then, without evaluating this answer, ask for another possible consequence. The child might then say, "He might cry." Pushed for another consequence, he might say, "He might hit me back." After thinking of a number of consequences, you might ask your child to think of consequences for another solution: "What might happen next if you offer to trade one of your toys for the toy you want?" The child might say, "He might give it to me." Another consequence might be "He won't want to trade." You can then ask your child, "Which solution do you like best?" If your child chooses a solution with a consequence that would hurt another child, you can ask him to think about how his friend might feel if he did that, helping him see another consequence of that solution.

The immediate goal of problem-solving instruction is not to put children on the spot to solve real interpersonal problems, but rather to help them think about how problems can be solved. You'll have better success doing this initially when tempers aren't flaring in the middle of a fight. Make problem solving a game that can be played with puppets, dolls, or role-playing. You might tell the children that these two stuffed

SCIENCE TO TAKE HOME

Youngsters who can recognize that behavior has causes and consequences, that people have feelings, and that there is more than one way to solve everyday problems that arise with others have fewer behavioral problems than those who merely react to the problem at hand. These children are less easily frustrated, less likely to fly off the handle when things don't go their way, less aggressive, and also more caring about others, more likely to share and take turns, and better able to make friends (Shure, 1994).

bunnies are arguing because they both want to play with the video game. Ask the children to think of many different solutions. Then ask them to consider many different consequences of these solutions. Then ask them to choose the solution that they think would work best for the bunnies. Playing this kind of problem-solving game often gets children in the habit of evaluating the impact of their solutions on themselves and others. This seemingly simple thinking skill takes a long time to develop, but it forms the core of a problem solving skill that will serve your children well throughout their lifetimes.

Parenting to Build Problem-Solving Skills

- Teach your child that the first solution that comes to mind when you have a problem is not necessarily the only or the best way to solve that problem.
- Encourage your child to think of alternate solutions when she has a problem.
- Ask your child to consider the consequences of his solutions.
- Let your child choose the solution she likes best.
- Practice problem-solving skills with play games and with puppets.
- Teach your child *how* to think, not just *what* to think.

Avoid

- Letting your child get in the habit of crying, grabbing, and hitting to solve problems.
- Expecting your child to know how to solve his problems with other people.

REMEMBER

Children can learn to diffuse hostility and avoid conflict if they are taught how to consider alternative solutions and consequences before they act.

- Asking your child to think about a good solution to a problem when she is in the middle of a tantrum.
- Solving all your child's problems for him.

Play and Imagination

Six-year-old Brittany lives in a world her parents call "Barbieville." Brittany has 14 Barbie dolls and all the paraphernalia that goes with them: the four-foot tall house, the pool, the car, the whirlpool, the limousine, the vacation resort, the food, the dog, and (oh, yes) the wardrobe. "Brittany would sit in her room with those dolls all day, if I let her," says her mom. "She just loves to dress and undress them and then move them from place to place."

Imaginative play is still an important part of the day for children ages 6 to 9, but its focus is changing. Instead of dressing up as pirates, superheroes, or rescuers, now children become the directors of these characters. The little peg people of earlier years are exchanged for more realistic dolls and action-adventure heroes. The child manipulates the actions of these figures and mentally writes the scripts of creative plots and schemes. Many of the play scenarios will recount episodes of television cartoon and adventure shows. Others will maneuver racing cars, space stations, and battlefields.

Costume play is less frequently seen in this age group, but it's not completely abandoned. Even at this age, pretending to be someone else still plays an important role in psychological development. When chil-

---

CONSIDER

Action figures are often popular with children this age. Their adventures usually involve bashing heads together, smashing bodies onto the floor, and even flinging enemies across the room. You may feel your children don't need this kind of aggressive stimulation. But remember: All children have aggressive and violent impulses that need expression. Action figures give them an opportunity to vent these feelings in acceptable ways. Certainly, you can use adventure play activities to suggest nonviolent ways to solve conflicts. But if you prohibit all forms of violent fantasy play, a child's aggressive nature may stay bottled up and may eventually be acted out in real-life situations.

SCIENCE TO TAKE HOME

Is there play after kindergarten? Judging from the relative number of studies of school-age and adolescent play as compared to play during the preschool years, one might come to the conclusion that children stop playing after they enter the first grade. But in fact, play continues to be an important element in the lives of children beyond the preschool years, and it continues to mirror their overall pattern of intellectual, social, and personality development (Hughes, 1995).

dren transform themselves into characters who portray images of success, strength, and power, their egos receive a positive boost. Children can also gain mastery of their fears by dressing up and acting like the characters that terrify them in real life. Becoming a monster or the grim reaper on Halloween, for example, gives children complete control over the character's actions and desensitizes them to its scary appearance. At this stage of development, dress-up can also help children establish their separate self-identity. By taking on the role of another in play, children gain a reflection of themselves as different from, but related to, other people. And finally, dress-up is still just plain fun. These good feelings lift spirits and act as buffers against the boredom and stresses of everyday life. So although your child may not dig into the family dress-up box as often as he or she used to, don't throw it away yet—there's still part of your child that loves to be somebody else!

Around age 8, a child's imagination becomes increasingly internalized into private thought and reveries. Mental images will meander along at length with an inner voice commenting on new experiences and feelings. Children this age will mentally rehearse athletic and play experiences; they'll replay school activities; they'll practice dialogues with friends and parents. This fascination with daydreaming can be maddening for parents trying to keep a child focused on a task, but when this happens, don't become overly concerned. This new internal world is just as captivating (and beneficial) for your child as were the overt make-believe games of earlier years.

When children begin to abandon their pretend world, they become more interested in board games and sports. Their developing sense of patience and the ability to understand and follow rules make games like Monopoly and checkers less frustrating than they were before. Children's new ability to understand the feelings of other children

JUST A PHASE?

There are many children who play video games occasionally and are not at risk for the problems associated with video addiction. But what if the games they choose are violent? Is this a cause for concern?

Look at the kind of violent games your children are playing. The ones that depict slayings and disembowelment of realistic human figures are not recommended. Real people killing real people models behavior that we don't want our children to consider fun. These types of video games should be banned in all our homes. On the other hand, the ones that involve battles between fantasy or cartoon characters serve the same function of releasing aggressive feelings as earlier play with action figures. In moderation, violence between imaginary beings will be found in the play of most children. Try to balance such play with plenty of nonviolent games and other social interactions.

allows them to show a sense of sportsmanship, and their increased attention span helps them enjoy sport practice sessions.

Parenting to Encourage Play and Imagination

- Remember that play is still an important part of the day for children ages 6 to 9.
- As your children outgrow their preschool dolls and toys, offer them more realistic dolls and action-adventure heroes.
- Accept that aggressive play with action figures gives children an opportunity to vent violent feelings in acceptable ways.
- Encourage your children's dress-up play; pretending to be someone else still plays an important role in psychological development.

Avoid

- Prohibiting all forms of violent fantasy play; this can cause children's aggressive nature to stay bottled up without an acceptable outlet.
- Discarding costumes for dress-up play too early. Children ages 6 to 9 still will occasionally like this kind of imaginative play.
- Allowing your children to play video games that depict slayings and disembowelment of realistic human figures.

REMEMBER

Play continues to be an important element in the lives of children beyond the preschool years, and it continues to mirror their overall pattern of intellectual, social, and personality development.

Language Development

After the age of 5 or 6, children develop a fuller appreciation of language. They expand their knowledge of word meanings and relations, and they refine their use of proper grammar. They continue to improve in their articulation of sounds, they enlarge their vocabularies many times over, and they further refine their understanding of relational terms, such as *follow* as opposed to *lead*.

Their growing understanding of language now allows school-age children to understand that sentences can have more than one meaning. Researchers asked children to explain how sentences like "The doctor is out of patience (patients)" can be interpreted in more than one way. They found that the ability to detect these differences first appears between the ages of 6 and 9. Children's awareness of lexical ambiguities (in sentences like "He did not have enough dough (money)") shows a gradual, steady improvement with age. But it is not until around the age of 12 that children understand that written or oral language can often be interpreted in more than one way, such as in sentences like "The duck is ready to eat," or "He saw a man eating fish" (Hughes, Noppe, & Noppe, 1996). Keep this in mind if your children seem confused by something they hear or read; they do not yet fully have the ability to understand the ambiguities of language.

Reading and writing are natural outgrowths of the child's growing language capacity. Arguably, the major language-related accomplishment during middle childhood is the development of the skills associated with reading and writing. Both reading and writing are forms of symbolic communication that involve, among other things, attention, perception, memory, and association with past knowledge and a particular context. That's a lot of information for young people to put together.

While children spend much school time practicing the skills of reading and writing, it has not been found necessary or even helpful for parents to drill their children on these skills at home. Social interactions between children and their parents, siblings, and friends set the groundwork for literacy acquisition in a much more important way than does merely mastering units of written language.

Parents can do much to encourage a positive attitude in their children toward reading. You can help your child acquire literacy basics in the following ways:

SCIENCE TO TAKE HOME

Because exposure at home to reading material and conversation forms the base for a child's literacy, researchers have begun looking at the language environments in homes. Betty Hart and Todd Risley, of the Juniper Gardens Language Project, found dramatic differences in the language environments of children raised in low-income, middle-class, and professional families. Low-income parents spoke to their children less frequently than did middle-class and professional parents. By age 5, the low-income children had smaller vocabularies (Azar, 1995).

- *Read.* Let your children see that you enjoy reading books and newspapers. Show them that you value reading as a source of enjoyment and information.
- *Stock up on reading materials.* Make sure there are plenty of books, magazines, and newspapers around your house.
- *Read to your children.* Don't stop story hours or bedtime reading now that your children are learning to read for themselves. Continue to read to them so they can enjoy the sound of language and the storyline without slowing down to sound out the words.
- *Talk with your children.* Conversation offers opportunities for vocabulary enrichment and language exploration.
- *Encourage diversity.* Encourage experiences like dramatic play, drawing, painting, music, and dance that (like reading) emphasize symbolic representation.
- *Allow for experimentation.* Let your children scribble and engage in nonphonetic writing with invented spelling. For fun exploration, this kind of creative writing is not wrong. It is a pressure-free way to play with language.
- *Encourage your children to read.* Make reading a part of every day.

Parenting to Encourage Language Development

- Play word riddles with your children to help them recognize that words can have more than one meaning.
- Provide social interactions between children and their family, siblings, and friends to set the groundwork for literacy acquisition.

- Remember that exposure at home to reading material and conversation forms the base for your children's literacy.
- Take an active role in encouraging a positive attitude in your children toward reading.

REMEMBER

The major language-related accomplishment during middle childhood is the development of the skills associated with reading and writing.

Avoid

- Expecting your children to have a full understanding of the ambiguities of language.
- Drilling your children on reading and writing skills at home.
- Expecting the school to instill a love of reading in your children.

Family and Peer Relationships

Children ages 6 to 9 switch their attention from family-centered to school-centered activities. It's no wonder that peer relationships become so very important. Children's developing social skills and the ability to understand the feelings of others now help them build friendships within a tight group of peers. This is a time for slowly pulling away from the family in an effort to be like everybody else. But it is also a time when family routines and rituals still give these children a sense of security, safety, and family closeness.

Building Friendships

Mara's mom was worried. "She's only 8 years old; I just think that's too young to be involved with a small clique of friends. She should be more open to lots of different people and opportunities."

Of course we want our children to be kind and friendly to all the children in their environment, but school-age children are bound to form small-group ties. Developmentally, these groups are a way of trying to make sense of the social order and figure out where one fits in. Many children will form "clubs" that require hours and days to set up and establish membership rules, even though the club itself rarely gets off the ground. This exclusivity is perfectly normal behavior.

Now is also the time for best friends. You'll quickly see, however, that a child's definition of *best friend* is probably different from your own. Close ties in middle childhood are frequently broken, mended, and changed within hours. By making and breaking relationships, children concentrate more on the form than on the content of friendships and, in a sense, are practicing how friendships work.

It's in these close friendships and small groups that secrets are shared (and usually betrayed) and gossip thrives. Gossip, too, is a developmental step–it allows children to concentrate on the exploration of the similarities of each group member, reveals attitudes and

AGE DIFFERENCES

Grade-school children have mostly same-sex friends. One survey showed that about 36 percent of all best friendships cut across gender among 3- and 4-year-olds, but this drops to 23 percent for 5- and 6-year-olds and becomes nonexistent for 7- to 8-year-olds (Kaplan, 1991).

CONSIDER

Children who are unpopular are likely to have deficits in social skills. They do not interact well with other children, criticize others, or are aggressive.

beliefs that the members share, and often involves criticizing other children. As children gossip, they affirm their norms and the values of the group.

Through these years, children will often weave in and out of friendship groups as they redefine what they need in a friend. Children this age tend to choose a friend based on shared interests as well as on the observation of who is fun to play with, who shares, and who doesn't. These are social skills that directly affect a child's popularity.

By the age of 6, children are less egocentric and less aggressive–making them better able to be a good friend. They are now able to understand the feelings and actions of others and resolve conflicts in nonaggressive ways. Children who learn prosocial behaviors (such as showing comfort, sympathy, sharing, and cooperation) make and keep friends more easily than children who are weak in these skills and tend to be more aggressive or withdrawn.

Although being the most popular child in class is not necessarily vital to achieving happiness and success, it is important that your child feel acceptance from peers. Research shows that children who are socially isolated are more likely to be low achievers and dropouts and to suffer from emotional difficulties. Isolation during childhood is serious business. For this reason, you should help your child learn the prosocial behaviors that promote friendships:

- *Teach your child how to be friendly.* It's not enough to say, "You have to be nice." Be specific: Teach her to smile, share, and say thank you.
- *Encourage prosocial behaviors at home.* If your child habitually talks in a loud and demanding voice, explain to him how to speak nicely. Then respond to his demands by simply saying, "When you ask nicely, then I'll answer your question."
- *Play by the rules.* Children who don't follow the rules are not accepted by their peers. If you consistently bend the rules of the games you play at home so your child can win, you're setting her up for ridicule and isolation on the playground. School-age children don't bend the rules for anybody, ever, even if they throw a tantrum. So get tough, and help your child accept and follow the rules of the game.

JUST A PHASE?

Your child may need the help and intervention of a psychologist, psychiatrist, or clinical social worker if you notice any of these trouble signs:

- **Your child has no friends at school, at camp, in sports, and so on, and the situation has persisted for over a year.**
- **Your child's mood plummets because of difficulties with peers.**
- **Your child's difficulties with peers cause stress problems such as depression, sleep difficulties, behavior problems, not wanting to go to school, or failing in school.**
- **Your child shows a pattern of being either a bully or a scapegoat.**

- *Share friendship stories.* Tell your child about your childhood friends. Share stories about breakups and makeups. Let your child know that his social struggles are common and that you understand.
- *Praise prosocial acts.* Behaviors that are noticed and rewarded are often repeated. When you catch your child using good social skills, reward her with praise, a hug, and a smile.

Parenting to Help Children Develop Friendships

- Understand that school-age children tend to form small friendship groups.
- Remember that it's normal for school children to change best friends on a regular basis and gossip about each other.
- Teach your child prosocial behaviors (such as showing comfort, sympathy, sharing and cooperation) so she can make and keep friends.
- Be alert to the signs of peer isolation.

Avoid

- Allowing your child to be aggressive, loud, and demanding with other children.
- Evaluating the quality of your child's friendships by adult standards.

REMEMBER

Children this age tend to choose friends based on shared interests as well as on the observation of who is fun to play with, who shares, and who doesn't. These are social skills that directly affect a child's popularity.

- Letting your child act aggressively and rudely at home. He will probably do the same with his friends, and they will reject him for it.
- Ignoring your child's social problems.

Family Rituals and Routines

Through all the stages of development, routines and rituals give children a secure anchor to home. They promise that home is the one place where family, traditions, and love are guaranteed, secure, and stable.

We strongly believe that parents need to establish routines that regulate bedtime and homework behavior for children this age. School children who are allowed to fall asleep whenever and wherever they happen to drop usually have significant school problems due to daytime fatigue. We have also found that arguments over homework assignments can be avoided when routines are used.

Seven-year-old Erin cries at the mention of the word *homework*. "Every night there's some kind of homework battle," moans her dad. "I'm about ready to give up the fight." Some parents do feel like they need a whistle and a bullhorn to get their kids through nightly homework. But because homework will be a part of your child's education for the rest of her years in school, now is a great time to establish homework routines that will get the work done and take the pressure off both of you.

SCIENCE TO TAKE HOME

Researchers at the Oregon Social Learning Center advised students to engage in specific daily home-study routines and asked parents to monitor and reinforce these efforts. At the end of the study, students reported significant improvement in homework quality (Forgatch & Ramsey, 1994).

You can help your child develop good study habits by helping him choose where and when to do homework and by encouraging him to use the selected place and schedule *every* school day. Enlist your child's help in setting up this routine. This shifts the responsibility for doing homework onto the child, and gives him a greater sense of independent accomplishment.

First, decide on a special homework place. It can be an isolated alcove or right in the thick of things. But whether it be in the kitchen, the dining room, the hallway, or the bedroom, make sure your child is comfortable and agrees that each day's homework will be done only in that place.

Then decide when to do homework. Consider your family's schedule, your child's preference, and the time it usually takes to complete assignments. Pick a time that's most convenient for everyone, and then stick to it. Consistency is the most important element in developing a homework routine.

You might include in your routine some family rules that help your child get the job done. No television until homework is finished, or no friends until the work is done are examples of clear-cut rules within the homework routine that can motivate children through their assignments.

CONSIDER

Even when there's no homework assigned, stick to the homework schedule. This time can be used for silent reading, review, or study to keep the routine going.

If your child still resists the homework routine after a few weeks of consistent enforcement, reevaluate the time and place. Maybe she needs time to exercise or relax before jumping back into schoolwork. Maybe he needs to be nearer the family or further away from noise. Don't hesitate to adjust your routine until you find one that works. Then one day you'll be surprised to find that the routine has turned into a habit. Your child will sit down at the appointed time and place, open her books and begin to work without your prodding, coaxing, or pushing. On that day you'll know your child has a most valuable educational tool—an independent work habit.

Rituals, too, can serve to give school-age children a sense of security as well as a special link with family members throughout the growing years. Many families share rituals around major holidays like a birthday, baptism, wedding, or anniversary. But you can also create unique rituals that are practiced and understood only by you and your children. Take homework, for example: Simply serving lemonade and popcorn after 15 minutes of work is a nice reward that can quickly become a tradition your child will look forward to. Anything you do at a predictable time can become a ritual for your child:

- Bring your child with you when you run Saturday morning errands. End the trip every week with a stop at the bagel shop and a cup of hot chocolate.
- Go out for a fast-food dinner and ice cream every Friday.
- Go for a walk every Sunday evening.
- End each school year with a party—balloons, cake, and all.
- Always say goodbye with a hand squeeze.

JUST A PHASE?

Persistent, compulsive rituals such as repeating actions over and over, washing hands continuously, or saying good night 20 times at bedtime may be signs of an anxiety disorder that needs professional assistance.

CONSIDER

Rituals are good for parents, too. Your good intentions to spend time with your children, to tell them they are special and important, and to pass on family values are often neglected in our busy world. Rituals make you schedule time to slow down and enjoy your family.

Rituals needn't be elaborate. Even the simplest of rituals can give children two things of great value:

- *A sense of identity.* Rituals help children understand what it means to be part of your family and who you are together.
- *Comfort and security.* Children are drawn into the arms of a family that uses little rituals to show them that their family is something special.

While consistency is important, rituals must also be flexible. You need to be aware of which parts of your rituals remain meaningful and which might be altered. If your child no longer wants to squeeze your hand when he says goodbye, maybe it's time to substitute the squeeze with a wink or a smile. If your child no longer likes popcorn with her homework, switch to another type of snack. Don't get hung up on the details and insist that traditions can't be broken. Bend the rules to fit everyone's needs as your children grow and change. The important thing is to offer beliefs, traditions, and a sense of order that your children can fall back on when the outside world seems cold and disordered.

Parenting to Create Rituals and Routines

- Remember that a set bedtime for school-age children is very important.
- To avoid arguments and procrastination, create a routine schedule for homework.
- Create unique rituals that are practiced and understood only by you and your children.
- Be flexible with your rituals; change them as your children's needs change.

Avoid

- Allowing school children to fall asleep whenever they want and wherever they happen to drop.
- Reserving family traditions only for major events like holidays and birthdays.
- Refusing to change the details of a ritual as your children outgrow it.

REMEMBER

Routines and rituals promise that home is the one place where family, traditions, and love are guaranteed, secure, and stable.

Peer Pressure

Eight-year-old Craig came home from school in tears. "No one likes me," he cried. "Teddy made fun of my shirt and everybody laughed. I hate this shirt and I'm never wearing it again." Wiping his tears, Craig's mother tried to reassure him, "That's a very nice shirt. You wear it and ignore those cruel kids."

But Craig can't ignore his classmates. This age group is marked by an intense concern about what others think. A social hierarchy begins to form and each child scrambles to find a place, always hoping to be liked by everyone. Many children will twist themselves out of shape in a desperate effort to fit in. Although you should continue to encourage individuality and nonconformity, keep in mind that children who are different in any way–whether because of physical characteristics, personality traits, manner of dress, or material possessions–can be excluded from social groups and cruelly taunted. Unless the in-group is engaged in destructive behavior, try not to get worked up about your child's sheeplike mentality–it's developmentally normal.

SCIENCE TO TAKE HOME

By the age of 5 or 6, children become increasingly peer-oriented and decreasingly family-oriented (Hughes, 1995).

At the same time, school-age children need to learn how to resist peer pressure when the stakes of personal safety are high. If you expect your child to say no when alcohol, drugs, and sex emerge onto the scene, the lessons in peer resistance must begin now. If your child defends a dangerous activity (like riding without a bicycle helmet or swimming in unguarded areas) by saying, "Everybody else does it," that's the perfect opportunity to work on peer-resistance training. Send the message loud and clear that a dangerous action doesn't turn into a safe one just because everybody is doing it. Help him use the problem-solving skills explained earlier to look at the possible consequences of a dangerous action and make the smart choice himself.

You can also help your child practice the decision-making skills that protect her from negative peer pressure by playing the what-if game. Each of you takes a turn answering a what-if question posed by the other person. You might ask, "What if a friend dared you to write your name in spray paint on the school wall?" Then, without pressure or fear of punishment, you and your child can discuss this kind of pressure situation.

You can also insulate your child against the dangers of peer pressure by keeping the lines of communication open. Let him know that

CONSIDER

Peer pressure is not always bad. Peer pressure can also have positive effects:

- ***It can be motivating.*** **A need for peer approval can motivate children to strive to be the best—in school, in athletics, or in music, for example.**
- ***It teaches useful social skills.*** **To have friends, children must learn how to share, wait their turn, and listen to others.**
- ***It teaches children about themselves.*** **Seeing themselves as other people see them helps children recognize their strengths and work on their weaknesses.**

if he should be swayed by friends to do something wrong, he can tell you about it without worrying that you'll explode. (Then promise yourself that you'll work on controlling your emotions when you hear bad news.) Tell your child, for example, that if she is goaded into stealing some candy that she should tell you what happened so you can help her learn how to handle the situation in the future. Make it clear that you will listen to problems with an open mind and help to find solutions that the child is comfortable with.

Dealing with peer pressure is a lifelong task. Help your child get an early start in recognizing and avoiding this kind of conformity.

Parenting to Help Children Deal with Peer Pressure

- Encourage individuality and nonconformity, but keep in mind that it is developmentally normal at this stage to want to fit in.
- Send the message loud and clear that a dangerous action doesn't turn into a safe one just because everybody is doing it.
- Help your child use problem-solving skills to look at the possible consequences of a dangerous action and make the smart choice himself.
- Practice decision-making skills by playing the what-if game.
- Keep the lines of communication open.

Avoid

- Getting worked up because your child wants to look and act like everybody else.

- Allowing your child to participate in a dangerous activity because she says "Everybody is doing it."
- Assuming that all peer pressure is bad.
- Exploding in anger when your child tells you about a mistake he made.

REMEMBER

This age group is marked by an intense concern about what others think. A social hierarchy begins to form and each child scrambles to find a place, always hoping to be liked by everyone.

Personal Growth

The process of finding out who one is and where one fits continues throughout the school-age years. Children ages 6 to 9 create a sense of self that is closely tied to their sense of accomplishment in comparison to their peers. They strive to be the best and create a self-image based on their ability to succeed. They also continue to pull away from the family and seek independence. They want to feel competent and capable.

Sense of Self

There is a dramatic increase in a child's sense of self-awareness from ages 6 to 9. As they look outward, away from the family, these children build a sense of identity based largely on their accomplishments. Because children this age spend most of their waking time in school and in out-of-home activities, it's natural that this achievement-based identity is strongly influenced by how they compare to their peers. Most school-age children try very hard to excel in school, in sports, in scouts, in social activities, and so on in order to bolster their self-image.

The level of success or failure in these attempts dictates the way children view themselves. A child who earns good grades will see herself as a good student and will therefore approach her studies with a positive, can-do attitude. But a child who has met with school difficulties and has assumed the identity of a poor student is apt to give up easily when faced with a challenge. In the same way, children with a positive view of their physical abilities are more likely to join in and play games and sports with other children, while those who see themselves as physically inferior often refuse to play. This sets up a vicious cycle, because the more often a child backs away from opportunities to improve his skills, the weaker his skills become, reinforcing his self-image of inferiority.

SCIENCE TO TAKE HOME

Positive self-esteem is related to better adjustment in school, more independence, less defensive behavior, and greater acceptance of others. It is also associated with school achievement (Gurney, 1987).

Children who are naturally talented and quick to succeed have little trouble developing a positive sense of self. It's when a child faces a challenge that she needs her parents' help to feel good about herself. You can help your child constructively deal with the sting of failure by focusing on the effort, not the outcome. When your child is having trouble with a homework assignment or a school project, for example, show respect for her efforts by saying something like, "I'm really impressed by how hard your are working on this assignment." This way she can feel good about herself even if she doesn't get an A. If a child joins a sports team and finds he is not the star, you can refocus his feelings of achievement by commenting on something specific that he did very well (even if it's only the way he cheers the team on from the bench). When children learn that effort is just as important as outcome, they have many more opportunities to build a strong sense of self.

CONSIDER

One reason school-age boys and girls stay clear of each other is because of their own insecurities about their sexual identity. When their sexual self-confidence increases in adolescence and they are cognitively sure that associating with the opposite sex will not alter their gender, then they will be better able to enjoy friendships with the opposite sex.

At this age children identify, consciously and unconsciously, with one sex or the other. As their identity as male or female becomes established, they begin to adopt stereotypical behaviors. To assure his masculine identity, a boy will stick with other boys and participate in play that encourages competition, such as team sports and one-on-one competitions. Contests that determine who is physically stronger reinforce a boy's identity as a male. Girls, on the other hand, more often engage in activities that are less competitive and more nurturing. Two females, for example, may spend time fixing each other's hair or having intimate conversations that express concern for each other's feelings. Although these children are acting out the extreme stereotypes of their gender, this phase of development shows that they are aware of male and female differences and are trying to figure out what it means to be one sex and not the other.

AGE DIFFERENCES

When children were asked which of two pictures (male or female) was best characterized by each of several traits (for example, who gets into fights, who cries a lot) few 5-year-olds showed any trait knowledge, while 75 percent of the 8-year-olds and nearly 100 percent of the 11-year-olds exhibited clear knowledge of the sex-typed traits (Best et al., 1977).

Determining who one is and how one fits into the world is a big job that occupies much of a school-age child's time and attention. You can help your child see himself as someone good, accomplished, and loving by praising his efforts to acquire these traits.

Parenting to Help Children Develop a Sense of Self

- Understand that children's achievement-based identity is strongly influenced by how they compare to their peers.
- Remember that children's level of success or failure in their attempts to excel in school, in sports, in scouts, in social activities, and so on dictates the way they view themselves.
- Be alert for the vicious cycle that occurs when a child backs away from opportunities to improve her weak skills, thus reinforcing her self-image of inferiority.
- Help your child constructively deal with failure by focusing on the effort, not the outcome.
- Expect some stereotypical gender behavior at this age.

REMEMBER

As they look outward, away from the family, children ages 6 to 9 build a sense of identity based largely on their accomplishments.

Avoid

- Feeling shunned because your child now often looks away from the home to build an identity.
- Scolding or ridiculing your child when he falls short of success.
- Insisting that your child play with a member of the opposite sex.
- Worrying because your child adopts stereotypical gender behaviors.

Autonomy

Eight-year-old Kara was crying because she wanted to go to her friend's sleepover party–and she was crying because she also *didn't* want to go. She wanted to be like her friends, who thought staying away from home for a night was a wonderful adventure, but the thought of being away from home overnight scared her. Although gaining autonomy is a normal developmental task of school-age children, it's not always an easy one. Children this age want to be independent and on their own, but at the same time they're afraid to stray too far from the security of home. This push and pull becomes doubly hard when parents also are torn between helping their children gain autonomy and keeping them close in the safety of the home. Should Kara's parents encourage her to give the sleepover a try, or should they encourage her to stay at home where she's comfortable and safe?

If your children are to grow up as confident, independent beings, they need the courage to try new things and move away from the security of the family. This courage is more readily found when parents take two steps back and offer a safety net when children fall. To do this you have to get out of the habit of solving all your child's dilemmas. Letting children solve personal problems for themselves is the first step toward their independence. If your child decides not to practice piano this week, let him face the consequence at his next lesson. If a child who is normally conscientious about schoolwork gets lazy and decides not to do homework one night, let her feel the thrill of rebellion and then pay the price at school the next day. If your child doesn't want to eat dinner, let him go hungry for one night. Autonomy is all about making decisions and then facing the consequences of those decisions. Children don't ever have to face the consequences if somebody else is always making the decisions.

This solve-it-for-yourself-approach doesn't mean children don't need parental guidance. Kara's mother can be helpful by guiding her daughter to consider the pros and cons of her choices. Having a parent who is a good listener lets children think things through out loud. In this case, no one gets hurt no matter which decision Kara makes. Her mother can best help by leaving the solution up to Kara and then supporting that decision. If it turns out to be a bad choice (because Kara decides to go and then calls her mother at midnight wanting to come home), there's no real harm done as long as Kara's mother continues to support her. Kara will lose confidence in her ability to choose wisely for herself if her mother should say something like, "I knew you wouldn't make it through the night." The safety net of the family is there to praise children for making an effort and to encourage them to try again in the future.

The solve-it-for-yourself approach to autonomy becomes less appropriate when children want to try something that might be dangerous. Should you let your 9-year-old walk the 10 blocks to a friend's house alone? Should you let your 7-year-old son go to the public men's room alone? How much independence can school-age children handle? These questions have no right or wrong answers. Most often, the answer depends on the child and the circumstance. But there are general guidelines that can be followed when in doubt:

- *Put safety first.* If your child wants to do something that you believe he does not have the good judgment to do safely, don't hesitate to say no. First-graders, for example, rarely have the ability to cross busy streets safely by themselves. They are too easily distracted and too inexperienced to judge car speed and distance.

- *Find a middle ground.* If your child wants to take a major step toward independence, compromise by allowing a smaller step forward. If, for example, your daughter wants to walk to school alone, offer to let her walk alone the last two blocks (where you can still keep her in sight).
- *Adapt to the circumstance.* If your son wants to go into a public men's room alone, you might give him that freedom if you're in your local library, but decide against the idea if you're at a large city zoo.
- *Know your own child.* Make your decisions regarding autonomy based on how well your child handles situations of responsibility. If she can consistently follow directions and listen to instructions, she shows that she is ready for some freedom. But if she still can't remember to bring home the books she needs for homework, she probably isn't ready for too much responsibility.
- *Watch out for peer pressure.* Just because another child's mom lets him go to the movies without an adult doesn't mean you have to let your child do the same. Every family has its own ideas about freedom and independence for children. Make your decisions based on your best judgment and your child's unique needs and abilities.

Becoming an independent person is a gradual process with lots of false starts and many ups and downs. It's a difficult transition for children that is often just as tough on parents. But giving your beloved child the freedom to move away from the security of the home is an invaluable gift that feeds the growth of a confident and autonomous human being.

Parenting to Nurture Autonomy

- Remember that children this age want to be independent and on their own, but at the same time they're afraid.
- Help your child find the courage needed to try new things and move away from the security of the family.
- Try to take two steps back and offer a safety net when your child falls.

- Let your child try to solve personal problems independently before you step in.
- Allow your child the freedom to make some decisions and then face the consequences.
- Be a good listener who lets your child think things through out loud.
- Make your decisions regarding autonomy based on how well your child handles situations of responsibility.

REMEMBER

Although gaining autonomy is a normal developmental task of school-age children, it's not always an easy one. Children this age want to be independent and on their own, but at the same time they're afraid to stray too far from the security of home.

Avoid

- Solving all your child's dilemmas.
- Encouraging your child to always stay close to you and take the comfortable route.
- Ridiculing your child for making a wrong decision.
- Allowing peer pressure to influence decisions that involve your child's safety

Responsibility

Nine-year-old Todd has informed his parents that when he turns 17 he wants a red convertible. He says this as matter-of-factly as he might request an ice-cream cone. Welcome to the age of entitlement–a time when children feel they have a right to expect that things will be handed to them without any effort on their part. This attitude may sound cute in a 6-year-old, but it gets very tiring very fast. School-age children are old enough to learn that they need to contribute to the world they live in before they can expect to be rewarded. This is the time to help them learn the valuable lesson of responsibility.

Most households assign chores to each child, but that's only half the battle. It's very important that you make sure your children follow through and do what you've asked them. If they're supposed to put their soiled clothing in the hamper and they don't, do you pick it up off the floor and throw it in the wash? If they're supposed to clear their dinner plates from the table after a meal but run off before the job is done, will you take the time to call them back to do it? Or will you just do it yourself? Keep track of how often you let your children ignore their responsibilities. If it's often, this is a good time to get serious about expectations and consequences. As the dirty clothes pile up, your children will have to face the consequence of having nothing to wear to school. If you leave the dirty dishes on the table hours after all other dishes are washed, your children will concretely see the result of their lack of responsibility.

If your child persists in avoiding chores or arguing about doing his or her share of the work, don't give up! First, reevaluate the chore schedule. When a child knows she must make her bed every morning, this becomes part of the daily routine–not something she can "forget." If you'd like your child to sweep the kitchen floor each day, schedule it right into the day as you would a soccer practice: After dinner every night, the floor is swept. Having a scheduled chore makes work the expectation rather than the exception. Also, check to see if the chore schedule is reasonable. If your child has many other daily demands, such as homework and sports, music, or dance practice, he may balk at using up his "free" time on chores. Children do need daily down time, so make sure that being responsible isn't making them exhausted.

While you're arranging your child's chore schedule, be very aware of the attitude your family displays regarding work. If chores are assigned as punishment, your child will never connect the value of doing work as a kind gesture to help others. If you yourself grumble and complain about your workload, your child will quickly pick up that same negative attitude. If you bark out orders, your child will come to dread chore time. Chores don't have to be associated with drudgery and anger if you sit down with your children and explain their value. Have a family meeting to talk about the need for everyone

---

CONSIDER

School-age children should be held responsible for their actions. If they break a vase in the store, they should help pay for it with money they've saved. If they hurt another child on the playground, they should apologize and offer to get help for the child. If they break a neighbor's window, they should go with you to explain what happened. Running interference for your children to protect them from the consequences of their actions teaches them to be irresponsible.

---

to pitch in to keep a busy household going. Talk about the many things that need to be done (like gathering papers for recycling, feeding the dog, and setting the table), and give your children an opportunity to choose chores they'd like to do and the time of day they'd like to do them. Be positive and supportive during this meeting. Be sure your children understand that you need their help and that you appreciate their willingness to pitch in. Then be sure that you smile while doing your own chores.

JUST A PHASE?"

If your child demands to be paid for completing simple household chores, it is time to instruct the child about the responsibilities all family members have in order to lighten the family workload.

At some point in your chore discussions, the subject of pay will surely come up. Some families feel that children should receive an allowance based on the work they do around the home. Others feel that doing one's fair share is part of being a family and shouldn't be rewarded with pay. Many take a middle position, which we tend to agree with: Daily scheduled chores are done without promise of pay. Larger, out-of-the-ordinary chores (like helping to clean out the garage or closet) are compensated in some way—either with a monetary reward or with a trip to the movie or a pizza place.

Teaching children a sense of responsibility does more than distribute the burden of household chores. It equips them with a sense of reliability, dependability, and capability that will come in handy when they venture into the work world alone.

Parenting to Encourage Responsibility

- When you assign household chores, follow through to make sure your children actually do them.
- Let your children see the consequences of their lack of responsibility.
- Create a predictable daily chore schedule.
- Assess thc attitude your family displays regarding work.
- Give your children the opportunity to choose chores they'd like to do and the time of day they'd like to do them.
- Be positive and supportive when you assign chores.
- Smile while doing your own chores.
- Decide how your family will handle rewards for work well done.

Avoid

- Doing your children's chores for them.
- Assigning an excessive amount of chores that allow no free time in a child's day.
- Assigning chores as punishment.
- Grumbling and complaining about your own work.
- Feeling you must bribe your children with money or other rewards to get them to do their assigned chores.

REMEMBER

Most households assign chores to each child, but that's only half the battle. It's very important that the children act responsibly by actually doing the chores. School-age children are old enough to learn that they need to contribute to the world they live in.

Character Formation

School-age children gradually learn the rules of right and wrong, and their developing sense of conscience helps them follow those rules even when no one is around to punish or scold. The way they think, act, and feel about issues labeled *good* or *bad* undergoes an almost constant reformation as they head toward adolescence. This is also the time when family discipline becomes a major concern. At this age, children constantly test the limits to determine exactly how much they can and cannot get away with. They also may start to "forget" how to be mannerly. Peer and media pressure tells them that crudeness and arrogance is cool. But loud and direct messages from home can counter these influences and help children grow to be confident, kind, and considerate young adults.

Values and Morals

Most school-age children between the ages of 6 and 9 still understand morality as a matter of simple obedience. The rules of life are absolute, unquestionable, and sacrosanct. Morality is based on someone else's authority and therefore is external to the child. But during this stage, children gradually learn that there is more to right and wrong than just following the rules and staying out of trouble. Physiological changes in the brain between the ages of 6 and 7 allow children to begin to draw moral distinctions based on internal judgments. While a 5-year-old will worry that his mother will be angry because he broke a vase by running in the house, a 7-year-old will feel guilty about breaking the vase because she disobeyed her mother's instructions. Children this age are also feeling the first pangs of a conscience. This is the depository of all they are learning about their family's values and standards. Occasionally, this conscience will send them a clear signal when they betray what they know to be right. This shift from doing what's right because of the presence of an adult and fear of punishment to doing

CONSIDER

No one would ever suggest that television viewing is a good way to learn the morals and values of our society. But it may not be directly to blame for the lack of morals and values, either. In their book *Bringing Up a Moral Child,* Michael Schulman and Eva Mekler tell us:

> **No program is going to be powerful enough to alter your child's basic values. How a program affects him will depend very much on the kind of person he was when he first sat down to watch it. If he cares about people, he'll dislike a program that promotes questionable morals as much as you will (Schulman & Mekler, 1985).**

what's right based on internal standards of conduct is the basis of moral behavior.

Children this age begin to see that the rules can sometimes be flexible. They come to see that what is *fair* is more important than what the rules say. They also learn that *intention* can dictate what is right and wrong more than the action itself. Now they may have a vague understanding that the child who breaks five dishes by accidentally dropping them is not as "wrong" as the child who intentionally breaks one dish by throwing it on the floor. They also begin to see that intention dictates the difference between a lie and a mistake. If asked, for example, if the mathematical problem 1 + 1 = 5 is a lie, a 5-year-old will insist that it is, because it is wrong. A 7- or 8-year-old will realize that it's only a mistake because the intention is not to deceive.

You'll notice your child's internal sense of morals and values growing in three distinct and yet interrelated areas: cognitive, behavioral, and emotional.

- *Cognitive.* Your child is learning to make judgments about what is right and what is wrong and to consider someone else's viewpoint.

JUST A PHASE?

If your child seeks out a steady diet of violent television programs (which have been associated with aggression in some children) or consistently identifies with the villain instead of the hero, this is reason to be concerned about the direction of the child's moral development. Monitor your child's television exposure, talk often about the feelings and needs of others, and if the behavior continues, seek professional guidance.

This major leap in thinking skills is related to higher levels of prosocial reasoning that prompt a person to offer sympathy, understanding, concern, and love. Lessons in the way one thinks about morality continue to be learned through experience, observation, imitation, and direct instruction.

- *Behavioral.* Learning to think about what's right and wrong is followed by behaviors based on that knowledge. Moral development is practiced every time a child's behavior (such as lying, cheating, impatience, and the inability to resist temptation or control aggression) is discouraged because it is *bad.* It is also developed through the encouragement of behaviors labeled *good,* such as acts of kindness, generosity, sympathy, sharing, and cooperation.
- *Emotional.* The emotional aspects of morality are the feelings one has after engaging in a particular behavior. Even when there is no one around to see a child misbehave, he will begin to feel guilty about it. This feeling can lead a child to confession and a need for reparation. On the other hand, the child who is able to restrain herself from doing wrong or participating in an antisocial behavior even when no one is looking will sense a feeling of personal satisfaction. These two internal feelings guide children in the process of moral development.

AGE DIFFERENCES

Age-related differences in children's understanding of consequences and intent are well established. Children younger than age 7 rely primarily on consequences when evaluating another person's actions. Children older than 10 or so rely on intentions. Between about 7 and 10, children rely on either one of these (Ferguson & Rule, 1982).

Parents teach their children about values and morality in direct and indirect ways every single day. Take some time to see if the lessons you are teaching your children are the ones you want them to learn:

Teach by example. If you tell your children that honesty is important, be honest. Hearing you tell the store clerk that you are returning an item because it is defective when in fact you simply changed your mind teaches children that honesty is important only when it doesn't inconvenience you, cost you money, or get you into trouble.

CONSIDER

Social learning theorists believe the family is the most influential factor in a child's moral development. Parents decide which social stimuli the child is exposed to and what the child is taught. They determine the categories of behavior that are defined as *good,* and therefore rewarded and encouraged, and those labeled *bad,* and therefore punished and suppressed.

Explain the reasons for your own moral decisions. If you decide to send money to a charity, show your children that you're doing so and explain why. If you prepare a dinner for a sick neighbor, tell your children what you're doing and why. This isn't bragging; it's teaching children how people take care of each other.

Don't overreact to broken rules. Your school-age children are just learning the difference between right and wrong. If you explode when they make the wrong choice, you may teach them to lie in the name of self-defense. Instead, remain calm and allow your children to admit their mistakes and learn how they can right them.

Use television violence to teach your children about moral implications. Talk about why a character got angry and wanted to hurt someone. Talk about the intentions behind a character's actions. Ask your children to suggest other ways characters might resolve their conflicts without using violence.

Give children opportunities to practice putting the family values into action. Too often parents pay lip service to certain values and their children see the hypocrisy in talking about things they don't actually do. Make an effort to participate in community activities such as food drives, clothing collections, and other outreach programs that show your children that your family cares about other people and does something to help those less fortunate.

Teach values through direct, targeted lessons. Talk about character-building ideals and be clear about your convictions. Use moral stories and appropriate moral lessons from events and lives. For example, if you want to teach your children about kindness, compassion, and their opposites, read stories like Charles Dickens's "A Christmas Carol." If you want to teach your children about persistence, tell them about the Little Engine That Could. If you'd like to emphasize the value of honesty, tell them about Abraham Lincoln, who walked three miles to return six cents, and, conversely, about Aesop's shepherd boy who cried wolf. These are all great stories that teach moral values we all share. They give children specific, common moral reference points.

SCIENCE TO TAKE HOME

Researchers Walker and Taylor (1991) have found that the parental discussion style that predicts the greatest moral development in children entails a high level of supportive, representational interactions. The representational category includes behaviors such as eliciting the child's opinion, asking clarifying questions, paraphrasing, and checking for understanding—reminiscent of the Socratic style of questioning.

For most of this stage, your children will behave because they don't want you to be angry and they don't want to be punished. But all along they are slowly gaining an internal system of beliefs, values, and morals that will guide them through the coming years when they pull further away from you and need a self-directed moral map.

Parenting to Encourage Values and Morals

- Give your child opportunities to develop a moral sense through experience, observation, imitation, and direct instruction.
- Make your values very clear to your child. Help him learn what you consider to be right and wrong.
- Praise your child's attempts at prosocial behaviors; scold bad behaviors such as lying, cheating, impatience, and the inability to resist temptation or control aggression.
- Set consistent limits that apply to you also. If dishonesty is not allowed in your house, don't be dishonest yourself.
- Practice turning your values into action. Get involved in family activities that reach out to others.
- Use stories and literature to give your child examples of valuable character traits.

Avoid

- Expecting your school-age child to do what's right even when you're not looking.
- Allowing your child the freedom to determine what is good and bad; she does not have the moral experience to make this decision.
- Severely punishing a child who confesses a wrongdoing. The confession is a positive step forward in the development of a moral conscience.
- Banning all television shows that portray violence. Instead, use them to teach lessons about motives and alternatives.
- Giving lip service to values that your family doesn't practice.

REMEMBER

Children gradually learn that there is more to right and wrong than just following the rules and staying out of trouble. Physiological changes in the brain between the ages of 6 and 7 allow children to begin to draw moral distinctions based on internal judgments.

Self-Control and Discipline

Eight-year-old Luis was furious. His friends were sleeping over at Anthony's house, but he wasn't allowed. "Why not?" he yelled. "Because it's a school night," answered his mom. "But everyone else can. Why can't I?" insisted Luis. "I just told you why," said his mom. "But I want to!" he screamed. "I said, no!"

Scenes like this make it look like grade-schoolers have no respect for their parents when they openly defy authority and won't take no for an answer. But the reason for the outburst is not quite so devious. Kids this age need to assert their independence by testing the limits.

But this doesn't mean you should cave in to your child's anger and abandon your good judgment and family rules. It means it's time to remember the importance of setting reasonable limits about the big issues that are important to you and of sticking to them.

A well-set limit clearly and simply states two things: (1) the limit, and (2) the reason for the limit. For example, "You cannot sleep over at someone's house on a school night [the limit] because you need to be home to eat, bathe, do your homework, and get enough rest so you are not tired in school [the reason]."

CONSIDER

Children raised with authoritative discipline develop a greater sense of self-discipline than other children. In several studies, children who complied with adults' demands when adults were present, but not when they were absent, were more likely to have parents who used authoritarian discipline.

This kind of limit gives your child a sense of security by clearly establishing your expectations in advance. It also makes it easier to use the authoritative style of discipline that sets firm limits and expects much, but at the same time is supportive and respectful of the child's needs and interests. (See Stage 3 for more information on authoritative parenting.)

Consistency in establishing and enforcing limits greatly reduces the number of unending, angry arguments that are bound to pop up when your child believes there's a chance you just might change your mind. Don't waver when your school-age child says, "But everyone else is doing it."

When you talk to your children about the limits you've set, it's not always so much what you say as how you say it that conveys your full message. You can improve the expected degree of compliance in school-age children if you pay attention to the following aspects of body language:

- *Volume.* A loud, angry tone of voice can make children feel intimidated or frightened. Speaking too softly, on the other hand, may cause your child to disregard an important message. It is best to talk to your child about limits with a firm and commanding (but controlled) tone of voice.

- *Eye contact.* Eye contact is important to ensure you have a child's attention. Before stating a limit, say your child's name and look the child directly in the eye.
- *Physical distance.* Adults in our society generally stand about two to three feet apart when they converse with each other. They generally stand even closer to children. When you're discussing limits and rules, it is important that you be close to your child. If you yell out directions or reprimands from across the room, the message will be lost.
- *Undivided attention.* When you have something important to say to your child, turn off all distractions, including the television. Giving your undivided attention (and requiring your child to do the same) gives your message a sense of importance. You cannot effectively teach your child how to behave while cooking dinner or reading the paper.

Be attentive to the nonverbal messages you are communicating as your teach your children the external boundaries they need to develop an inner sense of self-control.

You can also increase your child's willingness to follow the rules with these simple tactics:

- Convince your child that he can behave. Do this by sending him positive messages, such as "I know you want to help out at home," or "I like it when you play so well with your brother." Paying attention to good behavior is likely to increase it.

SCIENCE TO TAKE HOME

After a divorce, parent-child relationships often change. The custodial parent, usually the mother, becomes stricter and more controlling, while the other parent becomes permissive and understanding, though less accessible. Both parents make fewer demands for children to mature, become less consistent in their discipline, and have more difficulty communicating with their children (Hetherington, Stanley-Hagen, & Anderson, 1989).

- If your child does not quickly comply with your wishes, give a positive and a negative consequence: "If you don't argue with me about sleeping over at Anthony's house, you can have a friend sleep over on Friday night. If you do argue, there'll be no sleep-over at all."

- Teach your 8- to 9-year-old child how to use self-talk. Encourage her to talk to herself when she's faced with a decision about behavior. She can remind herself, "It's not kind to push other people out of the way," and "It's wrong to be dishonest." This kind of self-instruction helps children resist misbehaving in tempting situations.

Parenting to Encourage Self-Control/Discipline

- Remember the value of setting reasonable limits about the big issues that are important to you and of sticking to them.
- Set rules that have two parts: (1) the statement of a limit, and (2) the reason for the limit.
- Give your child a sense of security by clearly establishing your expectations in advance.
- Pay attention to your body language when you talk to your child about his behavior. Consider volume, eye contact, and physical distance. Also give the child your undivided attention.
- Help your child learn to behave by noticing and commenting on good behavior and by teaching her what to say to herself when she's tempted to misbehave.

REMEMBER

Children this age still need to assert their independence by testing the limits. Consistently establishing and enforcing limits greatly reduces the number of unending, angry arguments that are bound to pop up when your child believes there's a chance you just might change your mind.

Avoid

- Letting a child talk you out of a reasonable limit.
- Using power-assertion methods of discipline, such as yelling and hitting.
- Talking to your child about the family rules while you're busy doing something else at the same time.
- Letting family problems, such as a divorce, change your established style of discipline.

Manners

As children spend more time with friends and less time with the family, teaching and enforcing a code of manners may begin to feel like an uphill struggle. During these school-age years, it isn't cool to be polite or mannerly, and family lessons in politeness are easily overshadowed by lessons in rudeness learned through the media. Watch any television sitcom and you'll quickly lose count of the number of ill-mannered behaviors the characters display. Crudeness and arrogance are in–and not just in the world of pretend. Children see their athletic heroes spit at umpires, shove opponents, and use foul language in anger. Teaching good manners today isn't easy–but it is possible.

Because examples of politeness are not easy to come by, you can't expect that your children will pick up good manners by themselves; you'll need to give detailed instructions. Saying "I want you to be polite to Grandma" won't work. Be specific by saying something like, "I want you to spend five minutes with Grandma before you run off to play. Ask her how she is feeling and tell her about your new school project." You'll need to use this direct, instructional approach to teach common courtesy in many everyday situations:

- Tell your child exactly what to say when making or receiving a phone call. Have your child practice saying something polite, such as "Hello, this is Dan. May I please speak to Bob?" Or, "Yes, my mother's home; I'll go get her" (and then going to find you without screaming, "Mommmmm!").
- At the dinner table, be specific about your expectations, not only for how to politely eat food (with elbows off the table and with mouth closed while chewing), but also for how to act: It's rude to squabble with siblings, reach across the table, talk too loudly, or rush away from the table without asking permission.
- Teach your child how to speak to others. At this age children can learn to use good eye contact and proper volume and to keep their hands away from their mouths while talking.
- Don't forget to insist upon thank-you notes. If the thanks are for a present, you might use an incentive approach: "You can have the present when you write the thank-you note."

SCIENCE TO TAKE HOME

In their book *The Media Equation: How People Treat Computers, Television, and New Media Like Real People and Places*, researchers Byron and Nass present the results of numerous psychological studies that led them to the conclusion that people treat some forms of media as real people. Their studies show that people are polite to computers (Byron & Nass, 1996).

Teaching manners is a long and slow process. Even after years of prompting and reminding, school-age children are bound to be forgetful on occasion. Seven-year-old Eddie, for example, was so excited about going on his school field trip that he and his friends ran out of the classroom, pushing past the teacher and slamming the door in her face. Even the most well-mannered children will have embarrassing lapses like this in their conduct. You can be sure that when kids in the lunchroom organize a burping contest, polite table manners are not on the menu. When holidays fill the house with cousins and friends, proper introductions are often lost in the shuffle. In fun and exciting situations, manners are easy to forget, so expect temporary setbacks. Kids with impulse-control or attention-deficit disorders especially will have difficulty remembering rules of courtesy.

When you see a lapse in manners, don't ignore it or overreact to it. If your child forgets a rule of politeness, try a humorous reminder: "I must be having trouble hearing today; I didn't hear a thank you." If the faux pas occurs in public or in front of your child's friends, don't embarrass the child with on-the-spot reprimands. When you're alone together, calmly go over what happened. Kids usually don't know when they're being rude, so explain exactly what went wrong and how to fix it. Don't just say, "I don't want to see that rude behavior again." Try: "You have to hold the door for people behind you so it doesn't close in their face."

To help your children remember their manners, try these simple strategies:

Use praise. Because kids this age need to feel competent and appreciated, they sometimes act on natural impulses to do polite things, such as offering some of their snack to a friend. You can encourage

---

AGE DIFFERENCES

As your children enter school they are still anxious to please and most often will eagerly try to be polite. As they grow, however, you may find that they try to put on a cool image by being rude. They will slouch in chairs with their feet up on furniture; they will roll their eyes as you talk to them; they will respond to you with sarcastic remarks. Although this behavior stems from a natural need to be less like you and more like their friends, it doesn't have to be tolerated. Let your children know that you do not accept rude behavior.

---

these kind and helpful acts by noticing them. Comment specifically on what impressed you: "It was very considerate of you to come into the house to say hello to Grandma," or "That was thoughtful of you to bring along an extra pair of skates for your friend."

Choose your battles wisely. You can't make your child remember all manners all the time. So choose the one or two that are most important to you right now and focus on them. When your child seems to have them under control, add a few more.

Review in advance. Before your child lands in a situation where you want polite behavior to be observed (such as when you're having guests for dinner), remind your child of the behavior you expect.

Be persistent. Manners are learned gradually over an extended period of time. Don't give up because your child repeatedly forgets to be polite.

Be polite. The example of your own manners will teach your child more than your instructions. Watch how you answer the phone, how you behave at the dinner table, how you treat the elderly, and how you speak to those who disappoint you.

CONSIDER

You can't discourage rude behavior by being rude. When your child forgets his or her manners, don't make a public scene of scolding the child. Wait until you can talk in private and explain the problem and your expectations for future behavior.

The emphasis you place on manners will have far-reaching effects. Far from being outdated, good manners are still the expected norm in our society. Sociological experts tell us that polite people have more friends, have greater success in business, and are generally more content with their lives. These things make the persistence that's needed in order to speak louder than the media well worth the effort.

Parenting to Encourage Good Manners

- Use a direct, instructional approach to teach common courtesy in everyday situations.
- Be specific when you teach good manners. A directive such as "Be polite" is too vague to mean anything to a child.
- When you see a lapse in manners, don't ignore it or overreact to it. Politely remind your child how to behave.
- Remember that teaching manners is a long and slow process. Don't get discouraged and give up.

- Use the example of your own actions to teach your child how to be polite.

Avoid

- Expecting that your children will pick up good manners by themselves.
- Expecting children to always remember their manners.
- Discouraging rudeness by being rude yourself.
- Giving up trying to teach good manners because your children repeatedly forget to be polite.
- Expecting your children to be polite on special occasions if they are not required to be polite in everyday circumstances.

REMEMBER

Because examples of politeness are not easy to come by in today's world, you can't expect that your children will pick up good manners by themselves; you'll need to give detailed instructions.

References

Adler, T. (1990, December). Melody is the message of infant-directed speech. *APA Monitor,* 9.

Azar, B. (1995, December). Parents help their kids learn to learn. *APA Monitor,* 20.

Barclay, L. K. (1985). *Infant development.* New York: Holt, Rinehart and Winston.

Baumrind, D. (1967). Child care practices anteceding three patterns of preschool behavior. *Genetic Psychology Monographs, 75,* 43–88.

Baumrind, D. (1968). Authoritarian vs. authoritative parental control. *Adolescence, 3,* 255–272.

Baumrind, D. (1971). Current patterns of parental authority. *Developmental Psychology Monograph, 4*(1, Pt. 2).

Best, D. L., Williams, J. E., Coud, J. M., Davis, S. W., Robertson, L. S., Edwards, J. R., Giles, H., & Fowles, J. (1977). Development of sex-trait stereotypes among young children in the United States, England and Ireland. *Child Development, 48,* 1375–1384.

Bhavnagri, N. P., & Parke, R. D. (1991). Parents as direct facilitators of children's peer relationships. *Journal of Social and Personal Relationships, 8,* 423–440.

Byron, R., & Nass, C. I. (1999). *The media equation: How people treat computers, television, and new media like real people and places.* New York: Cambridge University Press.

Casey, M. (1996). *Red lace, yellow lace: Learn to tie your shoe.* Hauppauge, NY: Barron's Educational Series.

Craig, G. J. (1996). *Human development* (7th ed.). Upper Saddle River, NJ: Prentice Hall.

Cummings, M. E. (1989). Children's responses to different forms of expression of anger between adults. *Child Development, 6,* 1392–1404.

Dixon, J. C. (1957). Development of self-recognition. *Journal of Genetic Psychology, 91,* 251–256.

Dunn, J., Brown, J., & Beardsall, L. (1991). Family talk about feeling states and children's later understanding of others' emotions. *Developmental Psychology, 27,* 448–455.

Eisenberg, N., Fabes, R. A., Shepard, S. A., Cuthrie, I. K., Murphy, B. C., & Reiser, M. (1999). Parental reactions to children's negative emotions. *Child Development, 2,* 513–534.

Ellis, E. M. (1995). *Raising a responsible child.* New York: Carol.

Emde, R. N., & Buchsbaum, H. K. (1990). "Didn't you hear my Mommy?" Autonomy with connectedness in moral self-emergence. In D. Cicchetti & M. Beeghly (Eds.), *The self in transition: Infancy to childhood* (pp. 35–52). Chicago: University of Chicago Press.

Fagot, B. I. (1978). The influence of sex of child on parental reactions to toddler children. *Child Development, 49,* 459–465.

Ferguson, T. J., & Rule, B. G. (1982). Influence of inferential set, outcome intent, and outcome severity on children's moral judgments. *Developmental Psychology, 18,* 843–851.

Flavell, J. (1986). The development of children's knowledge about the appearance-reality distinction. *American Psychologist, 41,* 418–426.

Forgatch, M. S., & Ramsey, E. (1994). Boosting homework. *School Psychology Review, 23,* 472–484.

Friedrich, L. K., & Stein, A. H. (1975). Prosocial television and young children: The effects of verbal labeling and role playing on learning and behavior. *Child Development, 46,* 27–38.

Frodi, A., Bridges, L., & Grolnick, W. (1985). Correlates of mastery-related behavior: A short-term longitudinal study of infants in their second year. *Child Development, 56,* 1291–1298.

Gemelli, R. (1996). *Normal child and adolescent development.* Washington, DC: American Psychiatric Press.

Grusec, J. E., Goodnow, J., & Cohen, L. (1977). Household work and the development of children's concern for others. *Journal of Developmental Psychology, 32,* 999.

Gurney, P. (1987). Self-esteem enhancement in children: A review of research findings. *Educational Research, 29,* 130–135.

Hartup, W. W., & Moore, S. G. (1990, March). Early peer relations: Developmental significance and prognostic implications. *Early Childhood Research Quarterly, 5,* 1–17.

Hawley, T. (1998a). *Ready to succeed: The lasting effects of early relationships.* Washington, DC: Zero to Three National Center for Infants, Toddlers, and Families.

Hawley, T. (1998b). *Starting smart: How early experiences affect brain development.* Washington, DC: Zero to Three National Center for Infants, Toddlers, and Families.

Healy, J. M. (1998). *Failure to connect: How computers affect our children's minds, for better and worse.* New York: Simon & Schuster.

Hetherington, E. M., & Parke, R. D. (1986). *Child psychology* (3rd ed.). New York: McGraw-Hill.

Hetherington, E. M., Stanley-Hagen, M., & Anderson, E. R. (1989). Marital transitions. *American Psychologist, 44,* 303–312.

Hoffman, M. L. (1963). Parent discipline and the child's consideration for others. *Child Development, 34,* 573–588.

Hughes, F. P. (1995). *Children, play, and development.* Boston: Allyn & Bacon.

Hughes, F. P., Noppe, L. D., & Noppe, I. C. (1996). *Child development.* Upper Saddle River, NJ: Prentice Hall.

Jersild, A. T., & Holmes, F. B. (1935). *Children's fears.* (Child Development Monograph No. 20). New York: Columbia University, Teachers College Press.

Kaplan, P. (1991). *A child's odyssey.* New York: West.

Kennedy, J. H. (1992). Relationship of maternal beliefs and childrearing strategies to social competence in preschool children. *Child Study Journal, 22,* 39–55.

Kessler, D. B., Dawson, P., et al. (1999). *Failure to thrive and pediatric undernutrition.* Baltimore: Paul H. Brookes.

Kindlon, D. J., & Thompson, M. (1999). *Raising Cain: Protecting the emotional life of boys.* New York: Ballantine Books.

Klinnert, M. D., Campos, J. J., & Sorce, J. F. (1983). Emotions as behavior regulators; social referencing in infancy. In R. Plutchik & H. Kellerman (Eds.), *Emotion: Theory, research, and experience* (Vol. 2). New York: Academic Press.

Kutner, L. (1994). *Toddlers and preschoolers.* New York: Avon Books.

Lally, J. R., & Gordon, I. J. (1977). *Learning games for infants and toddlers.* Syracuse, NY: New Readers Press.

Leonard, R. J. (1993). Requests, refusals, and reasons in children's negotiations. *Social Development, 2,* 131–144.

Lonigan, C. J. (1944). Reading to preschoolers exposed: Is the emperor really naked? *Developmental Review, 14,* 303–323.

Main, M., & Goldwyn, R. (1984). Predicting rejection of her infant from mother's representation of her own experience: Implications for the abused-abusing intergenerational cycle. *Child Abuse and Neglect, 8,* 203–217.

Marks, J. (1996, April 22). The American uncivil wars. *U.S. News and World Report,* 66–72.

Marshall, H. R. (1961). Relations between home experiences and children's use of language in play interactions with peers. *Psychology Monograph, 75* (5, Whole No. 509).

Morris, R. J., & Kratochwill, T. R. (1983). *Treating children's fears and phobias.* New York: Pergamon Press.

Noshpitz, J., & King, R. (1991). *Pathways of growth: Essentials of child Psychiatry: Vol. 1. Normal development.* New York: John Wiley & Sons.

Ounsted, M. K., & Simons, C. D. (1978). The first-born child: Toddlers' problems. *Developmental Medicine and Child Neurology, 20,* 710–719.

Piaget, J. (1968). *On the development of memory and identity.* Worcester, MA: Clark University Press.

Prentice, N. M., & Fathom, R. A. (1972). Joking riddles: A developmental index of children's humor. *Proceedings, 80th Annual Convention,* American Psychological Association.

Pritchard, A., & Appleton, P. (1988). Management of sleep problems in preschool children: Effects of a behavioural programme on sleep routines, maternal depression and perceived control. *Early Child Development and Care, 34,* 227–240.

Pruett, K. D. (1997). How men and children affect each other's development. Washington, DC: Zero to Three National Center for Infants, Toddlers, and Families.

Ross, H. S. (1982). Establishment of social games among toddlers. *Developmental Psychology, 18,* 509–518.

Rutter, M., & Garmezy, N. (1983). Developmental psychopathology. In P. H. Mussen (Ed.), *Handbook of child psychology* (Vol. 4). New York: John Wiley & Sons.

Schaefer, C. E., & DiGeronimo, T. F. (1992). *Winning bedtime battles.* New York: Carol.

Schulman, M., & Mekler, E. (1985). *Bringing up a moral child.* Reading, MA: Addison-Wesley.

Shure, M. (1994). *Raising a thinking child.* New York: Henry Holt.

Smith, D. (1979, March). Puppetry and problem-solving skills. *Young Children,* 4–11.

Stayton, D., Hogan, R., & Salter-Ainsworth, M. (1971). Infant obedience and maternal behavior: The origins of socialization reconsidered. *Child Development, 42,* 1057–1069.

Stevenson, M. B., Leavitt, L. A., Thompson, R. H., & Roach, M. A. (1988). A social relations model analysis of parent and child play. *Developmental Psychology, 8,* 101–108.

Stifter, C. A., Spinard, T. L., & Baungart, R. J. (1999). Towards a developmental model of child compliance: The role of emotion regulation in infancy. *Child Development, 70,* 21–32.

Thelen, M. H. (1979). Treatment of temper tantrum behavior by means of noncontingent positive attention. *Journal of Clinical Child Psychology, 8,* 140.

Tyson, P. (1999, July/August). Taking a stand. *Sesame Street Parents,* 89–91.

Walker, L. J., & Taylor, J. H. (1991). Family interactions and the development of moral reasoning. *Child Development, 62,* 264–283.

Whitehurst, G. J., Falco, F. L., Lonigan, C. J., Fischel, J. E., DeBaryshe, B. D., Valdez-Menchaca, M. C., & Caulfield, M. (1988). Accelerating language development through picture book reading. *Developmental Psychology, 24,* 552–560.

Index

F

G

H

I